# IN THOSE DAYS

Francie - Sandy Run   c. 1932

# IN THOSE DAYS

✦

## Tales of a Happy Childhood
## 1926–1940

## *Frances Cheston Train*

For Frank —
Some early memories for you
much has changed, but
The Cheshire Co landscape has
been preserved — (P.99)
Very best
Francie
Thanksgiving 2015
(PS I have a book on "Friendfield"
called "A Carolina Plantation
Remembered" (from amazon.com))

iUniverse, Inc.
New York  Lincoln  Shanghai

# IN THOSE DAYS
## Tales of a Happy Childhood 1926–1940

iUniverse books may be ordered through booksellers or by contacting:

iUniverse
2021 Pine Lake Road, Suite 100
Lincoln, NE 68512
www.iuniverse.com
1-800-Authors (1-800-288-4677)

ISBN-13: 978-0-595-40968-6 (pbk)
ISBN-13: 978-0-595-85326-7 (ebk)
ISBN-10: 0-595-40968-7 (pbk)
ISBN-10: 0-595-85326-9 (ebk)

Printed in the United States of America

This memoir is for the dear memory of my mother and father; my sisters and brothers; my widely extended family then and now; my husband John; my children Alix, Whitney, Frances, and Harry; my grandchildren Josiah, Will, Chessie, Thomas, Whitney 3rd, and Harry Jr.; and to the memory of my devoted nurse, Margaret.

*As for you few remaining friends*
*You are dearer to me every day.*
*How short the road became*
*That seemed to be so long.*

Anna Akhmatova

# Contents

# Acknowledgements

Without constant coaching into the mysteries of word processing by my expert and patient teachers, Tom Tutor, Jim Mayers, and Sonia Dobson, I would not have been able to compose these happy memories. The Furman Printers in Bedford Hills saw me through many versions, with special thanks to Paula Kornbrust. My editors Fergus MacIntyre and Mark Donovan pulled the scattered vignettes into shape, and I was encouraged to continue by my agent Marianne Strong, and by my many friends who understood life "in those days." Thank you.

# 1

## *Sandy Run Farm*

I was born on July 22, 1926 and brought up on Sandy Run Farm, Oreland, Pennsylvania, a small village near the town of Fort Washington in Montgomery County, Pennsylvania.

Sandy Run was originally called Emlen House after its first owners, an 18th-century farming family. Solidly constructed from Pennsylvania fieldstone, the oldest part of the house was built before 1730. In the Revolutionary War, it was General Washington's headquarters for six weeks, while his troops were stationed first at Camp Hill, and later at Valley Forge, during that fierce December of 1777. In the march from Camp Hill to Valley Forge, the cracked and frostbitten feet of the starving American soldiers left bloody footprints in the frozen drifts.

Over nearly two centuries, the house had been enlarged to the big, rambling home where I grew up. There were eight family bedrooms with baths in the front part of the house, and the maids' quarters were in the "back hall," seven small dreary rooms, where some of the "girls"—parlor maids, waitresses, and kitchen maid—doubled up, two to a room. Each little room was furnished with a bureau, a straight-backed chair and iron bedsteads. Jenny, my mother's sweet lady's maid; Miss Smith, the English governess, a stuffy stiffly-corseted woman who always wore pince-nez fastened on a golden chain; the all-important cook; and my Scottish nurse Marg, were deemed superior beings on the domestic totem pole and therefore had their own modest, but more comfortable single rooms.

The property consisted of about thirty acres of fields, woods, extensive lawns, flower gardens, orchards, and vegetable gardens. There were kennels, stables, garages, and berry patches: neat rows of black currants, red currants, raspberries and gooseberries. The leaves of the plump green and white striped gooseberries were perennial targets for the despised Japanese beetle, a beautiful shiny green and black beetle with prickly black legs that clung to your hand when you picked the luscious tart fruit.

There were also beehives. I kept a safe distance away from the hives with their energetically buzzing occupants, which looked and sounded dangerous to us children. George Schumm, our patient head gardener, was also the beekeeper. He told us he didn't mind the stings because the bee venom helped his arthritis. Once from a safe distance, I watched while he collected a swarm. First, he smoked them with a metal teakettle-shaped smoker. The bees gathered on his chest and his face, and to my fascination he looked as though he wore a long, brown, buzzing beard. The bees even seemed to know him, humming to him by name: "Schummm." He taught me about what went on inside the mysterious hive. Several unborn queens are stored in special cells inside the hive, and when the old queen dies, or outlives her egg-laying years, the worker bees choose a new queen, and stroke her awake with their specially manufactured royal jelly. Before she soars off on her nuptial flight to mate with one of the eager drones, her first task is to go through the hive and murder all her rival unborn queens! It's not too different from the royals of yore (or even, perhaps, today).

Sandy Run had a big rambling stable with eight box stalls, unoccupied in the 1930's, but useful for housing any mournful female dogs in heat, or rabbits left over from Easter, or one of our exotic pets like the ocelot. The horses had been moved up to the farm at Unionville, Pennsylvania where my parents went foxhunting every season with Mr. Stewart's Cheshire Fox Hounds. Connected to the stable were two carriage houses, which later became garages.

The chauffeurs who took care of our cars were George Burns, an elderly red-faced Irishman who had been my mother's coachman, and the younger, mischievous Tommy Dunn, a wee Scot. They lived in dark, damp back rooms in the garage. Mr. Schumm and his assistant, Dominick Pierre, tended the grounds. They lived in Oreland, a village about a mile away, and walked to work early each morning, and trudged home again each night. Custom provided that the head gardener and head chauffeur were always called more formally by their last names, but underlings were called by their first names.

The cook, laundress and kitchen maid wore cotton-print housedresses, bib aprons, lisle stockings and "sensible" shoes. The housemaids were given uniforms suited to their station in the household: in the morning, long-sleeved sky-blue cotton dresses, with starched white collar, cuffs and apron. Their evening uniforms were more formal, either black or maroon silk, with a white apron.

The maids had alternate Thursdays off, beginning after breakfast. On Sundays the Catholic servants were driven to Mass, but had to be back in time to prepare and serve lunch. The Protestants were driven to church separately. In the afternoons, naps were allowed, but someone always had to be On Duty to answer the door or the telephone.

It was the accepted routine, and there seemed to be few objections to work at night and on weekends. Many of our staff were Irish, who had emigrated to escape appalling poverty in their homeland. Being "in service" in the United States—in spite of the long hours and little time off—must have seemed an improvement over their dreadfully hard life in the "old country," and they sent much of their low wages back home to help their families.

Winnie Brogan, our housekeeper, was the head of the household staff, with the power and authority of a butler. Imagine a butler in petticoats, and there's Winnie Brogan. She dealt with domestic troubles so as not to bother "the Madame," my mother, whom Winnie adored. Mummy was too softhearted to deal with disputes among the help, and my father was apt to be cross, impatient and dismissive with the staff, so Winnie's orders were law.

Back in those days when silverware was actually made of silver, our pantry contained a huge iron safe, big as a bank vault, with shelves for holding the epergnes, trophies, ladles, candlesticks, tea and coffee sets, platters and ornaments. Winnie kept the combination to this safe. My mother trusted her completely, and often sought her comforting advice about personal problems, as well as how to deal with those of the help.

Daddy hated butlers, ever since one stole my mother's jewelry early in their marriage. He thought that butlers always drank and fooled around with the young maids, and he felt the house ran more smoothly if there was only one Big Boss: him! He held the key to the wine cellar, which was reached through a trap door in the pantry closet. It was exciting for me to follow him down the rickety ladder to the dimly lit cellar that smelt damply of alcohol, and to watch him choose from among the musty, cobwebby bottles. I don't think he knew a thing about wine, being almost a teetotaler, and anyway it was only served at grand dinner parties. Scotch, rye whiskey, and gin cocktails were the drinks of choice in those days, in our house at any rate, and those were served very sparingly. There was never a permanent bar setup, and all drinks were ordered and served individually to guests and family.

Sandy Run was a wonderful place to grow up. Rose vines climbed the white-washed stucco walls that enclosed the formal garden. A little stone playhouse sat off to one side, containing an early American bed with rope slats and a rock-hard horse-hair mattress, a spinning wheel (which I never could imagine how to operate), a rickety old table, and four chairs. There was a big stone fireplace at one end—just for show, because we were forbidden to build any fires when we were little, even in fireplaces—and a glass-fronted cabinet displaying a collection of cheerfully painted dolls' china for pretend tea parties. Some of the dolls' plates were stamped "Made in Japan," but others were real antiques culled from our grandmother's collections.

A long cutting garden produced dozens of varieties of flowers for picking, and the green lawns in spring were blanketed with drifts of daffodils. Beyond a stone bridge that arched over the millrace, lay a secret garden with a lily pond, bright with pink and white water lilies. Their heart-shaped leaves were perfect platforms for frog concerts. In the pond's center, a statue of the goat-footed god Pan piped away, ready to seduce any vulnerable maidens who might chance by. A low stone building, the springhouse, squatted by the edge of the stream, its mossy-shingled roof sheltered by towering, piebald-barked sycamores.

In the springhouse, clear icy springs ceaselessly swelled and bubbled up from the limestone bedrock. The farm's extra milk and cream were stored there in silver milk cans balanced on flat slabs, which projected from the thick stone walls.

The springhouse was a lovely cooling off place on hot, humid summer days. I often scooped palmfuls of achingly cold water, and laid a sweaty cheek along the sides of the misted, chilled milk cans.

In those days before electric refrigerators, we had iceboxes. A jolly iceman delivered huge squares of clear block ice three times a week. He wore an apron of waterproof leather over his shoulder, and he manhandled chunks with iron tongs, carrying his frozen, dripping burden from the back driveway into the pantry where the stainless-steel icebox waited.

The lower shelf of the icebox was made of wooden slats, allowing the melting ice to drip through into a large pan, which had to be emptied two or three times a day. All our perishable food was stored inside on steel bars.

The iceman's visits were a source of much cheerful banter among the help, especially the young kitchen maids. With little or no chance for any social life, they looked forward to his flirtatious attention. He was strong and muscular from years of hoisting the heavy blocks of ice, but he was not the only handsome delivery boy to cheer up the maids. All our groceries were delivered separately by vegetable truck, meat wagon, and Mr. Gillies' smelly fish wagon with the ice water dripping through its floorboards. After consultation with my mother right after her breakfast, the cook phoned in the orders to all the different stores, a task my mother despised. She hated thinking ahead, a trait I inherited, and she usually ended up saying desperately to the cook, "Annie, what do *you* think we should have?"

On the rare occasions I was taken along to the actual grocery store, I was in awe of the way the genial proprietor added up a foot-long list of charges on the back of a brown paper bag like lightning, using a pencil retrieved from behind his ear. No calculators in those days.

Our land had been a farm in colonial times. A man-made canal—the mill-race—branched off from Sandy Run Creek in the upper meadow, and marked the boundary between lawn and fields. A barely perceptible current carried the mill-race's muddy water to Spring Dell Farm, where the mill had once ground flour for the whole neighborhood. To this day, the nearest village is called Flourtown.

The stream was a favorite play spot for me—a small tomboy. Often my only human company was my vigilant Scottish nurse Margaret Smith—Marg. But through the years, there were always the dogs to play with: a motley succession of bedroom dogs, kitchen dogs, barn dogs, terriers, spaniels, Labradors, mutts, two old flop-eared, curly-coated Chesapeake Bay retrievers, dachshunds, my mother's corgis, and my very own disobedient Scottish terrier, named Black Douglas...or "Duggie" for short.

In the spring, mallards nested in the bushes on the banks of the stream, muskrats tunneled in the banks, and ducklings scooted along the surface in long feathered skeins, following their paddling quacking mothers, as they raced to escape the barking pursuit of the terriers. There were turtles, and water snakes too, which made barefoot wading in the soft, pillowy mud particularly scary when it squelched up between my toes.

One Christmas, the family gave me a small flat-bottomed boat, which I grandiosely named the *Indian Queen*. I imagined the little millrace churning into a Wild River of No Return, which I bravely explored in my canoe. On those summer days, I was either climbing trees, playing Tarzan, or paddling in the stream.

It was especially exciting in the early spring, when the water swelled the stream to the top of its banks. Then there was no need to paddle and pole—just steer with the flow, like Huck and Tom on the mighty Mississippi. Once I nearly drowned when a spring flood swept the canoe out of control. The swirling, brown water snatched me toward a stone bridge, and down to the culvert that tunneled under Pennsylvania Avenue, a paved main road. My big brother George had been watching from the bank, in fact cheering me on, and instructing me in that insouciant way of brothers who don't want to risk their own selves: "Paddle harder, paddle harder, steer for the bank!" My canoe capsized, I fell out into the racing stream and the *Indian Queen* fetched up against the bridge.

Poor Margaret, stranded in the field, was praying and calling in vain for help, the dogs were barking frantically, but George managed to grab me by my raincoat as I bobbed by. The force of the current pulled my rubber boots right off, and I squelched home across the sodden lawn in my stocking feet, rather pleased with my adventure and narrow escape.

The reaction of my parents was, as expected, not hugs and thank-god-you're-safe, but anger because of doing such a dumb thing. All of us got in trouble.

Bonne Mama and her twins
Minnie (Amanda) and Ellen (who died age 9)

My maternal grandparents, Alexander and Sarah Drexel Van Rensselaer, lived about a mile from us on the crest of Camp Hill, although it was all part of the same property. Their house, Camp Hill Hall, was an ugly stone castle-like mansion, turreted and crenellated, typical of 19th-century Philadelphia architecture. There were stables, greenhouses, a squash court, a coach house and a lovely tiled swimming pool. The hill commanded an extensive view over the valley to Chestnut Hill, the town where we went to school. My grandfather said when he was in the Chestnut Hill Hospital seven miles away, he could see the big house from his hospital window and wondered if he would ever go home again.

Our grandmother, whom we called Bonne Mama, was a motherly, unpretentious lady, who loved nothing more than having her large extended family for informal country picnics and tea parties, belying her image as grand dame of Philadelphia society. They saved large-scale entertaining for their big townhouse at 18th and Walnut Streets on Rittenhouse Square, in Philadelphia.

Her father, Anthony J. Drexel (1826-1893), my great grandfather, was a successful banker in the firm Drexel & Co., founded by his father, Francis. He amassed a large fortune and his philanthropy was widespread. He took on a young New Yorker, JP Morgan, as his partner, and the Philadelphia firm with bases in Paris and New York, with ties to London, became Drexel, Morgan. Drexel hated publicity of any kind and was remembered as "a man of singular modesty, who feared and shunned praise more than blame," according to his partner and friend George W. Childs. Mr. Morgan went on to found his own firm, stating that "Tony Drexel will never get anywhere, he's too damn nice."

He founded Drexel University in Philadelphia on the innovative premise that the children of the working classes should be able to study the new sciences of the day, and relate their practical application to business, industry and the home, following the student's own career objectives. To implement this, the student was required to spend more than one-third of his college life working for a salary, applied to tuition. He called this approach "co-op," or "earn as you learn."

The Drexels were extremely religious, and their niece, Katharine (1858-1955) became a Roman Catholic nun who devoted her entire life and $20 million inheritance to found mission schools throughout the west and south, for the benefit of Indians (Native Americans) and Negroes (Blacks). She made it a rule in her churches and schools that there be no segregated seating. She founded Xavier University in New Orleans, then the first Negro university in the U.S.—all this thirty years before the civil rights crusades. Pope John Paul II canonized her in 2000.

Saint Katharine was a shrewd businesswoman; she insisted that the nuns in the order of the Sisters of the Blessed Sacrament, which she founded, enroll in practical courses at Drexel University.[1]

Red Cloud - Oglala Chief

SAINT KAtharine Drexel
1858 – 1955

FOUNDER OF SISTERS OF The Blessed SAcramenT
for Indians and Colored  1891
Founder of XAvier University, The first
University for Blacks in The U.S.A.

---

1.   Rottenburg, Dan, *The Man Who Made Wall Street*.

It is to my deep regret that I was never taken to meet her. I would have been thrilled to hear her tales of the old West, where she became a friend of Chief Red Cloud, and to learn about her firm stand against the prevalent discrimination against Negroes. My family must have had some sort of anti-Catholic bias, but I never knew about its origin, and cannot understand it, especially since my mother's grandparents were such pious Catholics themselves.

The Van Rensselaers owned a beautiful steel, schooner-rigged, steam yacht, the *May*. She was built in 1891, 766 tons, 240 feet overall, with a 27-foot beam, and 14.5-foot draft. She had a crew of 40, counting the officers, the chefs, engineers, stokers and sailors. My mother's favorite among them was a young lad called McCoy, who later, in Prohibition days, became famous as the "importer" (smuggler) of the very best Scotch whiskey. McCoy's bootleg whiskey was so sought after, that it inevitably became known as "the real McCoy."

When the *May* sailed off to Europe, my grandparents took everyone along: their four children—my mother, her two sisters Mae and Minnie and younger brother, John—their governess, the tutor, John's little Cairn terrier, and a number of guests. The girls wrote a daily gossipy newspaper, called "JUST OUT," mostly about invented shipboard romances, and a talented guest artist painted watercolors of the scenes they encountered in the informal log of the voyage.

The yacht's interior was as luxurious as a palace, with working fireplaces, gas-fitted lights, paneled rooms, a book-filled library, formal dining room with silver candelabra, and silk brocaded bedspreads and curtains in the staterooms.

The Van Rensselaers cruised everywhere up and down the northeast coast of the United States. The yacht visited England, France, Egypt and even India. They usually left the children in Paris or London to attend school during their longer voyages, but once on a trip to Egypt, my mother was allowed to stay aboard. In a bazaar in Cairo, she secretly purchased a bandaged object that the street peddler told her was "the mummified hand of Queen Nefertiti." She was thrilled to possess such a valuable and unique souvenir, and successfully hid it in her bureau on the yacht until a terrible smell was traced to her stateroom. After unwrapping the bindings, the hand of the Queen was discovered to be the decomposing paw of a dog.

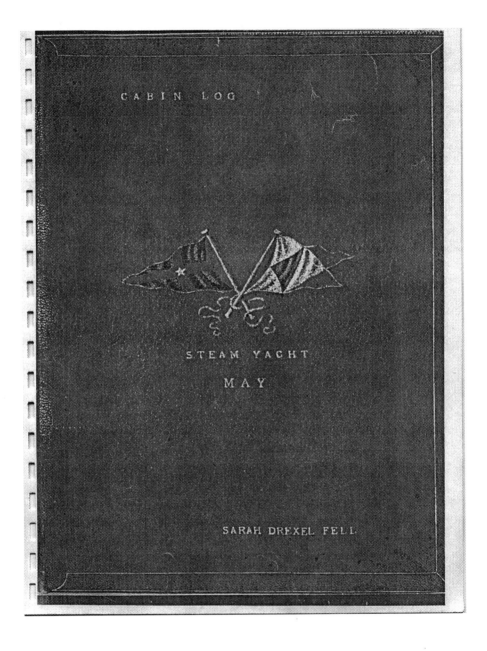

*The crew of the* May *and some of the passengers. Mummy is the girl in the white dress.*

MAY                                      ALEXANDER VAN RENSSELAER

At home, in Pennsylvania, my mother's sister Aunt Mae and her husband, Uncle Gouverneur (Gouvie) Cadwalader lived in a big Tudor style mansion called Hawkswell, about a half-mile down the hill from my grandparents. Our house was in the valley below. Spring Dell Farm, across the main road from our two driveways, was also part of the family enclave, so we never had to leave the property to have a fine excursion. We girl cousins went to the same school in Chestnut Hill. First we went to Miss Zara's, kindergarten through second grade, then to Springside, through eighth grade until boarding school. Gouvie Jr. went to the all-boys Chestnut Hill Academy.

Each morning at precisely 8:15, two big Packards would pull out of the gates of our adjoining driveways. Tommy Dunn, our family's chauffeur (never called "driver" in those days), always drove my nurse Margaret and me. The Cadwaladers' second chauffeur, Pat Gavin, drove my three cousins and their nurse Christine. Apparently, it never occurred to our parents to carpool. Gouvie was so embarrassed by being chauffeured that he often made Pat let him out a block away from school so his classmates wouldn't see his posh arrival.

His father, my uncle Gouvie, was a portly man with black hair parted exactly in the middle. He wore gleaming polished English boots, Harris Tweed coat and cap, and was content in his role of gentleman farmer, although he held an engineering degree. They had plenty of money to live as they liked.

He was a connoisseur of American furniture, and their house was filled with beautiful Philadelphia heirlooms, although we children were unaware of their value and rarity. My mother and Aunt Mae were not very impressed with such furnishings, and took them for granted, having been brought up surrounded by treasures of all sorts. For example, no one ever told me that the portrait of General Washington that hung over the fireplace in our hall was an authentic Gilbert Stuart. We weren't warned to treat antiques with special respect, except for the fascinating golden mantel clock in my aunt's library that chimed a tinkling tune and had a moving crystal waterfall, which we children were strictly forbidden to touch...no matter how urgently we wanted to discover if the "water" was wet.

My uncle was always kind but expected strict obedience from his children and me. My aunt was much more indulgent. She adored and spoiled her three children, my first cousins. Maisie was the oldest, famously beautiful and admired by legions of beaux. Next came young Gouvie, a handsome good-natured boy. Minnie, funny, plump and mischievous, was my age and my lifelong best friend.

We used to walk to Spring Dell Farm every weekend, shadowed by our two nurses. The four of us did everything together in our preteen years, since we lived so close to one another, and were isolated from any neighbors. We got along famously in spite of the keen competition between our nurses. Christine bragged that her charges were the best dressed, the brightest at school, the best looking. She was from the North of Ireland, and always a kind of pill, prissy and pretentious, while Marg was a funny and warm-hearted Scot. They were natural rivals.

Philadelphians, like southerners, set great value in family ties, and are intensely loyal, even to distant relatives. The blood-bonds are lifelong, and transcend the generations. My cousins and I remained as close during seventy years as we were when we were kids together.

My uncle would rap us across our bare legs with his walking stick if we made too much noise around his beloved Guernsey dairy cows; of course, he wanted to protect four chattering children from getting trampled or kicked by the cows.

I was scared that he might punish my naughty pup, Duggie, who liked to torment the huge mean dairy bull by darting under the pipe bars of his corral, nipping and barking at him. The bull would toss his head, slinging saliva, pawing at the ground. I was fascinated by the enormous sack between his hind legs, which swayed back and forth when Duggie taunted him, and I wondered what that ugly thing was...but I never dared ask.

We loved to visit the cool, spotless dairy where thick whole milk rippled in ivory streams over silvery chilling pipes, eventually to be separated into milk and cream, then stored in tall shining cans on the damp cement floor.

We drank the milk at home and if the full glass sat for a minute, there would be a float of yellow cream on the top (this way before Starbucks and the *latte* craze). I always drank at least four glasses a day, except in springtime when the cows ate wild onion grass and their milk tasted garlicky. Today, my husband says I have thick bones like a peasant. I could fall off a roof onto cement and bounce—all that calcium, I guess.

Besides the two giant workhorses Buck and Dolly, and the dairy cows, there was a stubborn burro that liked to bite. I remember nice brown hens, a ferocious rooster and a horribly smelly billy goat. Once my cousins and I tried to harness him to a rickety miniature hay wagon, but we couldn't make him pull it. He showed his stained teeth, butted at us with his gnarly horns, and glared at us with his strange yellow eyes with their horizontal pupils. We hated him. My brother told me that he was fifty years old!

Nearby was the old white-stuccoed farmhouse where Mr. and Mrs. Gordon—the head farmer and his wife—lived. The big Mill Pond lay close in front of the Gordons' house, and we skated there in the winter. It never froze completely, because of the current running through it from the millrace.

The three nurses—Margaret and Christine and Margaret Montgomery, the nurse in charge of our other cousins, Francis and Howard Gowen—would huddle in their long tweed coats, safely beyond the pond's edge, gossiping and stamping their black buckle galoshes, warning us ceaselessly with shouts of "Be careful!" "Don't go too far out!" "Don't go near the waterfall!" and the oft-repeated, "Stop it this minute, you limb of Satan!" These were directed mostly at the boys, who ignored the nurses' admonitions as much as they ignored the hand-painted sign warning "DANGER THIN ICE."

I don't remember ever enjoying the skating too much. In fact it was torture. I was apprehensive about the thin ice and the open water, and besides, Mummy never let me have new ice skates that fit. She thought it would be too extravagant, because I would outgrow them so quickly, and I was always afflicted with hand-me-downs. Either I wore a pair of my older sister's too-large figure skates, and skated miserably on my ankles, or else jammed my feet into a tiny pair of my mother's vintage 1928 size-fours. My toes froze instantly.

Then came the agony of attempting to undo yards of shoelaces with numb fingers, clumping about on the brown frozen turf or crusty snow on wooden block feet, feeling the needles jabbing my skin as circulation painfully returned.

Afterwards came one brave last try, jamming my feet back into the thin black leather skate boots, the steel runners cold as sword blades against my soles, despite too many layers of thick home-knit woolen socks.

The boys fared better. They had hockey skates and sticks, and would play vicious games, slapping great thumping whacks at chunks of wood. (No one bought pucks in those days.) As I wobbled across the ice in my secondhand skates, trying to keep up, the boys would come flailing and scraping toward me, arms windmilling, stopping inches away in a shower of ice spray, knocking me off my feet.

Howls! Howls from the nurses to STOP IT AT ONCE! Shrieks of rage from the sprawling girls, and tears from the youngest boy, who couldn't get up at all because he was so tightly swaddled in woolly clothes. Yips and yelps from the excited dogs, scrambling to join the fun, their claws digging into the ice as they tried to gain traction and steal the makeshift puck.

But salvation was at hand when Mrs. Gordon, a thin perky old lady wearing her usual flowered-print bib apron, called us into her cozy kitchen for the most delicious hot chocolate in the world, so sweet, dark and rich, with a spoonful of farm cream dissolving on the top, scalding our cold lips, and burning our tongues.

We thawed out in her kitchen, mittens steaming on the edge of the coal cook stove, our feuds forgotten, apple-cheeked and content. Then bundling up again, we would leave in the fast darkening afternoon, calling our good-byes, to walk homeward down the long rutted farm lane and up the driveways to our separate houses.

Another memory of Spring Dell Farm had its darker side. One summer day, when we were playing about the barnyard, we saw the hired man's twelve-year-old daughter, Bernice. There was something wrong with Bernice that none of us quite understood. Mental illness and retardation were never discussed in those days. She usually hid from us, but this day she came close, and tried to tell us something.

Bernice had a severe speech impediment, and we couldn't understand her words. She was cross-eyed, and had thick round glasses with steel rims. She wore a strange tam-o'-shanter pulled way down over her Dutch-girl haircut. Her garbled, guttural speech and her bizarre appearance disturbed and frightened us, and our fear made us giggle and whisper to each other.

I don't remember whose idea it was, but we decided to lure Bernice into our wonderful playhouse. It was a spooky stone building, built in late Victorian times for my mother and her sister Mae when they were little. It was always called "The House That Jack Built," and was supposedly strictly off-limits for us because of unsound floors. It was named after the familiar nursery rhyme:

> *This is the farmer sowing his corn,*
> *That kept the cock that crowed in the morn,*
> *That waked the priest all shaven and shorn,*
> *That married the man all tattered and torn,*
> *That kissed the maiden all forlorn,*
> *That milked the cow with the crumpled horn,*
> *That tossed the dog,*
> *That worried the cat*
> *That killed the rat,*
> *That ate the malt,*
> *That lay in the house that Jack built.*

A narrow spiral staircase curved up three floors, with a turret at the top. A real, wood-burning iron cook stove sat in the kitchen, goblin-size, and on the second floor was a wooden bed, Goldilocks and Baby Bear size, with sagging rope slats covered by a musty black and white ticking mattress. In the tower, behind a heavy wooden door with iron strap hinges, there was nothing. It was an empty room, with mullioned, spider-webbed windows waiting for one of Bluebeard's victims, or a desperate imprisoned maiden like our captive, Bernice.

We coaxed and pushed her to the top floor, slammed the door shut—but not locked—and ran down the stairs, leaving her whimpering and terrified, beating ineffectively against the thick walls of her prison.

I don't know how she found her way out, and no one discovered our secret cruelty. I suppose that some grownup heard her cries, but the poor little girl could never explain what had happened to her.

I only saw her one more time, when I ventured into the stone shed where her father and Mr. Gordon did their butchering. Bernice was standing behind the long bloodstained table where the pigs were cut up. A dead-animal stench filled the dank air.

Her eyes stared at me, like distorted and magnified marbles behind her thick glasses, and saliva glistened at the corners of her slack lips. *Did she recognize me? Did she remember?* I fled that awful room, ashamed and frightened.

Later I was told that the hired man had been let go, and we never heard anything more about him and his daughter.

I have harbored a lifelong uneasiness dealing with mentally retarded people, which most certainly stems from deep-seated guilt about the cruel trick we played on Bernice in the tower. I deeply regret the shameful and thoughtless game we played in that summer's childhood innocence.

# 2

## *My Family Circle*

My mother Frances Drexel Fell was born in 1887, and was married at a young age to Antelo Devereux. They had two children: Alix, born 1911, and Antelo Jr., born 1913. In 1919 her husband suffered severe brain damage resulting from a fall in one of the cross-country timber races in which he often competed. He was an accomplished gentleman jockey, often competing in the Maryland Hunt Cup—a four-mile race over rolling countryside, over twenty-two stiff post and rail fences. On two of his three wins, he was mounted on my mother's brilliant racehorse Scandaga. It is hard to exaggerate her love of horses and the outdoor life she cherished her whole life long.

My mother stayed by him through the next five years of his increasing mental darkness, followed by total amnesia. When it became apparent that he would never regain his memory of her, or of their children, she felt compelled to divorce him.

I believe this was a landmark case, the first time in Pennsylvania that a divorce had been granted for reasons of amnesia. Divorce carried a stigma in those days, and, for example, no divorced person was invited to the annual Philadelphia Assembly, a prestigious dinner dance that demanded white tie and tails, ball gowns and jewels. I doubt this bothered my mother. She was unimpressed by the trappings of society.

My father, Radcliffe Cheston Jr. who was born in 1888, married Sydney Ellis, before he went off to join the army in World War I. They had two children, George, born 1917, and Sydney, born 1918. Then tragedy struck this marriage also. Radcliffe's young wife joyfully traveled up to New York from her home in Bryn Mawr outside of Philadelphia, to meet the ship on his return from overseas. She fell ill in the hotel, and died within three days in the Spanish Influenza epidemic of 1918, leaving their two motherless babies.

That flu pandemic killed more than forty million people, a greater mortality than four years of the Black Death. At least 675,000 people died in America alone.

In 1925 my mother and father married. My father probably was delighted to leave the gloomy mansion, Fox Hill, presided over by Mrs. Ellis, his bossy and demanding mother-in-law. He had been living there since the death of his wife, and it was a great relief to move to my mother's cozy house, and to find happiness in her cheerful, unpretentious companionship and her generous acceptance of the obligation to raise two more children.

So, George and Sydney Cheston, accompanied by their strict governess Miss Smith, and a young Irish nursemaid, Peggy Quinn, joined my mother and her two children, Alix and Antelo Devereux, at Sandy Run. The four children became one family. And then I came along: July 22, 1926. With so many half-siblings, I wasn't really an only child, but I was often alone, except for the household help. My father and mother were away much of the time, and I was much younger than my four half-brothers and half-sisters. Sydney, nearest to me in age, was eight years older, but I was lucky to have those three Cadwalader cousins who were so near me in age and lived within walking distance.

My mother's oldest daughter—beautiful, sweet-natured Alix—was fifteen years older than me. By the time of my earliest memory, Alix had married and moved away. Her new husband was Rodman Wanamaker, of the merchant family who owned the department store…Wanamaker's.

My sister's marriage to "Roddy" would eventually end in divorce for "irreconcilable differences" (a euphemism of the day for infidelity). Years later, Mummy was trying unsuccessfully to correct the time on a beautiful tiny wristwatch that Roddy had once given her. Shaking her head ruefully, she said, "This watch is just like Roddy: terribly attractive, and totally unreliable!" Alix's daughter Minnie, my niece, was only six years younger than me, and she used to stay with us often. At the time I had a parrot, creatively named Polly, and it soon learned to imitate her.

The nurse would hear Minnie crying in an upstairs room, and would come rushing up to discover Polly having a fine time, slyly cocking his head and doing his realistic baby imitations. For years afterward we were treated to mournful sobs, howls and babble coming from the cage on the third floor. I was sort of glad not to have a little sister, if that was how they sounded!

My oldest half-brother Antelo was at St. Mark's School and Harvard during the 1930's, and only came home during the holidays. He was kind and funny and very good-looking. He took me for drives in his racy car, and one memorable night he let me watch him shoot rats in the local dump, sighting his .22 rifle with a headlamp. Antelo had cheerful handsome friends, and I followed them around as much as they could stand it, a pesky little kid sister. He was unfailingly patient and good-natured, and I idolized my big brother for the rest of my life.

George and Francie c. 1932

Next in age came my half-brother George, about nine years older than me. He was an unmerciful tease in his teen years, always in trouble with the family for sleeping through church, leaving his room a mess, playing the Victrola at ear-splitting volume, and trying unsuccessfully to teach my parrot to swear.

George was tall and lanky. I didn't realize it at the time, but probably the reason he hung around me so much when he was home from St. Mark's was because he must have been lonely at that stage of his life, and even then rebellious at the restrictions and narrowness of life within the confined Philadelphia society of that day.

Antelo was well behaved, humorous, a good athlete, and a popular and diligent student. George, bright and impatient, probably suffered by comparison, as he struggled with the usual teen problems. Daddy was very hard on him, and George took out his some of his frustrations persecuting and teasing me and Margaret, my beloved Scottish nurse.

I remember one night when my parents were out, how furious she became when he hooked up a dangerous series of flimsy extension cords from his own room, down the long hall, to the floor outside her locked bedroom door. There he planted his Victrola, forcing her to listen to a recording of Maxine Sullivan—a popular leather-voiced singer of the day—belting out a jazz version of "Loch Lomond." He played it over and over with the volume turned up full blast. This hurt her feelings, as she felt it was a direct insult to her Scottish heritage. "On the bonnie, bonnie banks of Loch Lomond" was a sacred song for her.

When I was about eight, George went through a Dracula phase. He told me that Count Dracula stayed buried in our dark coal cellar during the day, and emerged at night disguised as Margaret. He warned me not to let Marg kiss me good night, for then "she" would bite me on the neck and suck my blood, and turn me into one of his vampire slave girls.

The next night, poor Marg was distressed and puzzled by the strange behavior of her formerly loving little charge, and she was even more bewildered a few nights later when she came to my bedroom door and found a pile of mulberry branches, a clove of garlic, a mirror and a crucifix. I had learned from Bram Stoker's book that these were the only talismans that would protect me from the dreadful Count. George swore me to secrecy, and it was many terrified nights later before my parents discovered the reasons behind my strange phobias.

I looked up to George in spite of his vampires, even though he always found new ways to tease me, like the time he dared me to climb up the steep stairs to the hayloft above our garage. The room reminded me of an illustration in my book of poems by Eugene Field, of a spooky hayloft containing an enormous spider crouched in her web, ready to pounce.

In this loft there was a dark space between the floor and the sloping shingle roof, where I could only just manage to crawl under crisscrossing beams, and make my way out to a section where piles of dusty furniture and old trunks were stored. Behind these lurked a giant stuffed marlin, glaring with his fierce and predatory glass eyes, waiting to pierce me with his long sword-nose and eat me.

Those trunks always reminded me of the gloomy tale of "The Mistletoe Bough." In a Christmas game of hide-and-seek in a Scottish castle, Lord Lovell's young bride hid in an old chest in the attic. The lid closed down upon her, muffling her screams for help. She was not found until many years later, when some children exploring the attic happened to pry open the trunk. To their horror, her skeleton hand was still holding a withered sprig of mistletoe. I was always morbidly fascinated by scary stories like that.

Another time George scared me half to death when he climbed out the window of his bedroom, slid down the sloping shingle roof, and made his way hand over hand along the fragile gutters to my bedroom window. He hung there in the dark, making horrible snarling werewolf noises. He could have fallen to his death if the gutters had given way. I was too petrified by the "thing" at my window to call for help. Why did he risk his life to scare me? I'll never understand.

But, I sort of enjoyed this teasing, secretly relishing the attention from my big brother. In a strange way, these adventures forged a strong bond between us, as I managed to pass most of the tests of courage and loyalty without tattling on him.

My sister Sydney, unfailingly kind to me, was a shy, reserved, golden blond. I especially loved lying on her bed, watching her getting dressed in her party clothes, and hearing about her life and her glamorous friends from Foxcroft School.

Much later, during World War II, when George was a Lieutenant in the Navy, and Antelo a first Lieutenant in the Army—First Philadelphia City Troop, 28th Infantry Division—a scandal almost came into our family. Sydney and Antelo, stepsister and stepbrother, fell in love.

At the time, I was a nosy and romantic thirteen-year-old, and early on I realized that their feelings for each other were not quite those of a sister and brother. One day I happened to surprise them when I walked into a room unexpectedly, and was astonished when they sprang apart from an obvious non-sibling type embrace. But I never told on them. I loved them both wholeheartedly, and even more so when I discovered their secret, defending them staunchly to all the suspicious ones, especially my maiden aunt Lily who never thought it proper anyway that they had been brought up under the same roof as brother and sister. I remember telling Aunt Lil rather pompously, "Suspicions are like bats among birds, they ever fly by night," a phrase I had read somewhere.

Antelo had always respected my father and called him "Dad"…but now he had a dilemma. Although "Dad" was his stepfather, might others think that Sydney was his real sister? I doubt he really worried about it, as he had never been formally adopted, and after he requested his stepfather's permission to marry Sydney, everything was fine. Both parents were delighted. Amazingly they had never guessed what was brewing. I often wondered about the family rupture that would have occurred if the marriage failed, and my father's daughter divorced my mother's son. But they had a serene and happy life with few surprises, until Sydney died after forty years of marriage. They had two sons, my double nephews!

An age gap of many years separated me from my brothers and sisters, but our love for each other was close and enduring. I never experienced the sibling rivalries that many of my friends seem to remember, probably because of the big differences in our ages and life experiences. My mother, with her kind and generous nature, never took sides. She took great care to be fair and loving toward her motherless stepchildren, and my father always admired his beautiful stepdaughter and his quiet, gentlemanly stepson. My half-brother George told me much later that he always loved my mother as dearly as the image of the mother he had never known.

Except for the semi-isolation from school friends who lived too far away for easy visiting, I was cheerful and happy. It didn't dawn on me until much later that my parents were years older than the parents of my classmates. Mummy was 39 when I was born; her sister, Aunt Mae, was 42 when she had my cousin Minnie. This made a difference in their attitude toward child rearing, and probably explained why Minnie and I were left so often with governesses and nurses. After all, our mothers had already raised their much older children, and even had grandchildren by the time I was born.

In the diary I kept as a ten-year-old, the same entry appears many times: "Came home, did my homework, listened to the radio, went to bed, read my book. BORING!!" The biggest difference from one day to the next was which radio program I listened to. Very little parental interaction was ever recorded in my diary.

We children were never told a thing about the secrets in our family: I found out years later that my mother's brother, Uncle John Fell, had been murdered by the last of his many wives, while on his honeymoon. They were cruising on his grandfather Anthony Drexel's 279-foot yacht, *Margarita*, while visiting Java.

(She stabbed him at breakfast with a fruit fork, so the gossip had it. I guess the Drexels hushed up the murder, as there was no trial!)

I never knew that my mother's first husband had lived until the early 1940's in a nursing home, even though my mother and his two children used to visit him every month. When I was growing up, I didn't even know that Mummy had been (gasp!) divorced. I always thought Mr. Devereux had died before I was born.

My siblings and I were brought up under the stern motto of "never explain, never complain." I learned to turn the serious into a joke, and to conceal any troubles. I was expected to behave, be obedient, be polite, to see the other point of view, and above all, never to hurt anyone's feelings, and never question parental authority. Although this sounds as though I was a wimpy Pollyanna, I was actually a lively and cheerful tomboy. It was the characteristic Quaker attitude that permeated our Philadelphia society at the time. By today's standards, readers will wonder why my generation was so complacent, so accepting, so uncurious, but that's exactly the way it was for most of us brought up in that particular milieu.

Personal vanity was frowned upon. The family had a beautiful collection of Japanese netsuke ornaments, made of carved ivory. These were kept in a glass-fronted cabinet on the second-floor landing of our big front staircase. Once, when I was about twelve, I paused on the stairs to look into this cabinet, and I could see my reflection in the case's mirrored backing.

In the mirror, I saw my father coming up soundlessly behind me. "Who do you think you're looking at?" my father's reflection challenged me.

"No one," I whispered, and fled upstairs to my third-floor room, ashamed of...what? I didn't fully understand. Ever since that encounter, I am reluctant to spend much time in front of a mirror. It might be better if I did!

My entire life has been reflected in the looking glass of my cozy, happy childhood. Perhaps it left me lacking competitiveness, avoiding confrontation, and with few defenses against adversity, but it gave me valuable lessons and insights about understanding, trust and forgiveness; traits that have served me well over the years.

# 3

## *Mother and Father*

Franc in Drexel Fell Cheston
Mother

RADCLIFFE Cheston, Jr.
Father

On winter mornings Jenny, my mother's lady's maid, always kept to the same routine. Alert for the ring of Mummy's bell, between 7:30 and 8, she knocked discreetly on the door, and then slipped quietly into the cold, darkened bedroom. "Good morning, Madame, did the good Lord give you a lovely rest?" was her accustomed greeting, as she knelt at the hearth, lit the wood fire, then closed the windows and drew back the heavy chintz curtains.

While Mummy was in her bathroom, Jenny tidied the bed, plumped the three pillows in their linen cases, and laid out the hand-knit blue or pink bed jacket.

My father would already have woken up by then, and discreetly gone through a connecting door to his own bedroom and bathroom. My parents were born in the late 1880's and were raised under standards of extreme Victorian modesty. My mother would never use her bathroom if she thought her husband was even on the same floor. He might hear her flushing...or something even worse. "Did your father go downstairs yet?" she would ask me. I never saw them in the same bed together.

In fact, I rarely saw them kiss, or use endearments, yet I never questioned their devotion to one another. Arguments were kept private. "Not in front of the children or the servants" was the rule. This meant that table conversation was limited to the commonplace, and nothing private was ever discussed in public. Confidences were never shared with the children, nor were we encouraged to share our problems with them.

Mummy would come back from her warm bathroom, ready to eat a huge breakfast. She was about five feet tall, and delicately built, never weighing more than 104 pounds in her life, although she often complained about being too fat and needing to "bant" (diet). She had a strange machine hidden in a big closet that I loved to try out. You stepped on a platform like a doctor's scale, put a foot-wide rubber band around your hips and bottom, turned on the electric switch, and it was supposed to vibrate away those pounds.

In those days, the 1920's and 30's, my parents believed in English-style breakfasts, just as they believed in church every Sunday, and martinis made with equal portions of gin and vermouth (these were called, simply, "cocktails"). It was an Upstairs Downstairs household. Even the magazines, fanned out neatly on the library table—*Punch, The London Illustrated News, The Tatler,* and *The Field*—were British.

Delia, the parlor maid, carried up the heavy breakfast tray, laden with its flower-patterned breakfast china. It was a long trip from the kitchen: into the pantry, through the big living room, up the grand staircase, down the hall, and finally to the master bedroom. The back stairs were too long and steep for tray carrying.

At the bedroom door, Delia handed off her precious cargo to Jenny: coffee and hot milk, eggs or porridge with sugar and cream, bacon or scrapple. A rack of toast was supplemented by a pot of jam, or our own honey gathered by Mr. Schumm from Sandy Run's beehives. Jenny looked it over to make sure nothing had been forgotten, unfolded the morning paper, and vanished to straighten up the bathroom.

I ate breakfast downstairs with my father, in the big dining room. He was always dressed for the office, in a bankerly English tailored suit, with stiff collar and sober silk necktie. He barely spoke to me during breakfast, which he ate hidden behind his copy of the *Philadelphia Inquirer*. This was lucky for me, because it was awful to watch him eat his eggs. He ordered them boiled only three minutes, which left them so soft and stringy he could barely get them to stay in the spoon. Disgusting! I hated to hear him slurp, and even worse I hated the days when there was Cream of Wheat with a shiny skin, and lumps. I'd try to sneak out, but the command from invisible Daddy behind the paper always came: "Finish your breakfast, Frances, and kiss me goodbye. Have you done all your homework?"

One terrible morning I had a mouthful of hot Ralston cereal, when I suddenly sneezed, spraying a mouthful onto the back of Daddy's newspaper with a sound like rain on a tin roof. Luckily, my father was so absorbed in his reading that he didn't notice, and that time I went unpunished for gross table manners.

Normally, however, no one got away with anything when Daddy was around. He knew everything, noticed everything, and expected obedience from everyone. I cringed when he ordered Delia to take something back to the kitchen to be cooked again, or replaced. His voice was angry and peckish, and I felt sorry for the poor maid and the cook at her stove.

Every morning, in an unvarying routine, Daddy put on his grey fedora and grey tweed overcoat, and was driven to Oreland to catch the 8:30 Reading Railroad train to town. (Philadelphians never called it "the city.") He always walked from the station to his office, which was a mysterious place called Smith Barney. My father was a founding partner of the firm, but I didn't see his office until I was a teenager and I don't remember ever being curious about what he did "at work." Fathers didn't bring office matters home to the family in those days. Maybe that's what gave him a chronic ulcer—keeping so many worries bottled up, especially at the time of the 1929 crash, which I knew absolutely nothing about. Our life did not change an iota. I think he may have outsmarted the market, buying our shooting plantation in South Carolina before that terrible Black Tuesday.

He was even more in charge at Friendfield Plantation than he was at home. The men who worked for my father there used to say of him, with perfect truth: "The Boss can see a gnat on an orange, clear across the yard." Every day, during our stays at Friendfield, he would patrol the lawns, picking up strands of Spanish moss and small branches that had blown off the live oaks. He left these in neat piles to be picked up later, pointing them out to one of the men, or one of us children, with a jab of his walking stick.

My mother was just the opposite, easygoing and indifferent to such details. She would never complain about the service, or find fault with badly cooked food or minor, unintentional mistakes by the staff.

Daddy was a smallish man, with a round stomach and thick prematurely white hair. His face was pink, and he had large brown sympathetic eyes betraying a sentimental nature that he tried to hide by his gruff manner. I loved to bury my face in his rough Harris Tweed jacket, inhaling the smoky smell of the peat still lingering in cloth that had been woven in a cottage in the western isles of Scotland. I remember the smell of his hair tonic too, and the feel of his scratchy whiskers when he kissed me goodnight.

Although short-tempered, Daddy loved us all dearly and tried to be fair. He always expected the best from us, and wanted the best for us. He could be playful and funny when he felt like it, a mood we all cherished because of its infrequency. I was delighted by a verse he sometimes sang, to the tune of "The Battle Hymn of the Republic":

> *She wore her pink pajamas in the summer when it's hot.*
> *She wore her pink pajamas in the winter when it's not.*
> *And sometimes in the springtime, and sometimes in the fall,*
> *She used to crawl between the sheets, with NOTHING ON AT ALL!*

I thought this song was unbelievably racy and comical, especially from my stern Daddy! My mother also loved these times. Once, when he had consumed a couple of drinks—a very rare occurrence—he began acting silly in front of some lady friends of my mother's, and she was delighted. "See, Cliffe can be funny once in a while!" Mummy proudly announced.

He could sometimes be tough on me. His idea of a swimming lesson was to order me into my grandmother's pool, then to poke me forcibly away from the edge with the end of a long bamboo skimming pole while bellowing "SWIM!" The pool had no shallow end, and was usually freezing cold. If I tried to grasp the end of the pole, gasping and choking, he pulled it away and poked me some more. That was my swimming lesson. To this day I don't swim very well, or very far out.

I only remember being spanked by him once. I must have had a tantrum about something, and was howling obnoxiously, and the more he spanked, the louder I yowled. He said, "If you don't stop crying, I'll spank you again." He told me later that I sobbed, "How can I stop crying until you stop spanking?" My logic defeated him!

Mummy had sparkling blue eyes, a famously infectious laugh, an irreverent sense of humor, and a husky smoker's voice. She whistled like a music hall star, played jolly tunes and spirited hymns on the piano, and couldn't resist a practical joke.

Once, a family story goes, she was asked to a dinner where there were bound to be people she didn't know. She cut the eraser from a pencil, stuck a few hairs from our spaniel onto it, and glued it on her chin. For a while the guests were too polite to mention it. She often answered the telephone using foreign accents, just for fun. In fact she had such a deep voice that people often addressed her as Mr. and she rarely disabused them.

She loved the outdoor life, especially riding and fox hunting, and she golfed, sailed, hunted quail, shot grouse in England, and fished for salmon in Canada. There is a photograph of her, grinning from ear to ear, standing next to her Canadian guide as he hoists her record salmon, almost as long as she was tall. Yet she was equally at home in a drawing room or a grand dinner party.

After school, when she was expected home, I would wait impatiently, perched on the wide window seat at the top of the stairs, from where I could spy her car coming into the circular driveway in front of the house. Her arrival was always a treat, and I looked forward to every minute spent in her company. She and I always made time for cozy chats before school in her warm bedroom. She would be propped up on stacks of pillows, a good novel open by her side, with one or two Welsh Corgis on the foot of the bed, quivering in anticipation for more scraps of bacon.

I used to wonder if I could ever be a charming conversationalist like my mother, as I sat in tongue-tied silence at the dinner table, overcome by teenage shyness, but she never teased me or put me down, even when I felt self-conscious.

Like her own mother, she loved children, and used to get my friends and me in deep trouble with my father, by egging us on to laugh and misbehave. In fact, during one unforgettable dinner at Friendfield, Daddy, who hadn't gotten an in joke banished us all from the dining room, even my mother.

*Mummy and her big salmon.*

Bryn Mawr Horse Show c. 1920

We recovered some degree of composure in the library, and made our way sheepishly back to the dining room, where one look at my stern-faced, irritated father, sent us back out again, collapsing with the "church giggles."

Much later my mother was just as irresistibly comical with her grandchildren. When "Gramps" wasn't looking at her, seated down at the far end of the long decorated Thanksgiving table, she caught my six-year-old son's eye, pulled down the corners of her mouth and eyes, and stuck her tongue out at him. Everyone cracked up, even the waitresses, except the patriarch of course.

Mummy was an accomplished rider. She rode sidesaddle, always beautifully mounted on a shiny spirited thoroughbred, and on formal days wore an elegant dark blue habit, top hatted and veiled. The photograph on the previous page catches her sailing over a four-foot post and rail fence at the Bryn Mawr horse show, wearing her joyful confident smile. She and her two stylish cousins, Mary and Frances Paul, made up an unbeatable Hunt Team in many of the local horse show competitions.

Mummy was deeply loved by everyone; the maids, her grooms, fishing guides, storekeepers, dressmakers, friends of all sorts, dozens of male admirers, her vast extended family, especially her sometimes bemused husband, and all her children and stepchildren. She was always the witty life of any party, with her mischievous (and sometimes naughty) point of view. She charmed the men, as she was a great flirt and loved a double entendre, but she could always spot a phony, and was a penetrating judge of character.

Once a dashing, middle-aged friend of my grandmother's, a man named John Waddington, came to visit…and visit, and visit. He had a John Barrymore mustache, walked with a limp, and carried a nifty leather swagger stick. My father despised him, perhaps because he was so obviously attracted to my mother, and he remained openly skeptical of his tales of desert adventures. Despite his English name, Captain John de Penderill Waddington was a Frenchman. Mysteriously, he sometimes used the alias "Llanover," but no one ever discovered much about his past, except that he had been an officer in a Spahi regiment in North Africa. A drawing of him, wearing a pith helmet, and signed with a flourish, *Waddington*, had long been in our library in a fine silver frame. My father kept trying to displace it, to no avail. Mummy always returned it to a prominent spot.

Once Mr. Waddington stored some suitcases in the attic, much to Daddy's annoyance, for it clearly signified that he had plans to return. I happened to be there when he discovered them. Daddy was an incurable snoop, and he couldn't resist prying one open, hoping to find incriminating evidence of some kind. He pulled out a wide piece of khaki-colored flannel, and holding it up between thumb and forefinger as though it harbored fleas or cooties, he growled, "Typical of the man. A dirty kidney band." Kidney band? I found out later that it was a normal piece of clothing for desert troops, sometimes worn under the jacket to ward off fevers.

Mr. Waddington fascinated all of us cousins, and later, when he had bought a stone cottage near our farm in Unionville, we used to trek up there to have lunch a few times a year. He lived the frugal life of a bachelor, as though on a constant army bivouac. His lunch for us always consisted of sardines consumed directly from the can, which he passed around the kitchen table. Much later, surprisingly, he married a rich Frenchwoman, and after he died, it turned out he had always been rich himself!

Mummy's life was not idle. She was a faithful board member of the Seaman's Church Institute, and an enthusiastic member of the local garden club, "the Weeders." Every Friday afternoon she was driven to the Academy of Music for a concert by the Philadelphia Orchestra, and there were appointments for dress fittings, visits to relatives and friends and ailing pensioners, and perhaps an interview with prospective retainers.

My father despised orchestras (except on the radio), the opera, bridge players, the theater, art galleries and of course the ballet. (Those indecent tights!) My mother could never persuade him to take her out to the theatre, and they never, ever went to a restaurant, in those days.

Ladies didn't meet each other for outings then, except for luncheons at the Acorn Club, a women's club in Philadelphia. On the other hand, my father and his friends often lunched at their all-male clubs: the Philadelphia Club, Racquet Club, Fish House, and Rabbit. The outings to the latter two were all-day events, where the older members did all the fancy cooking, and the newcomers, called "apprentices," had to do the prep and washing up. You had to stay on as an apprentice for years, until one of the older members died. The food was memorable, and the "Fish House Punch" was lethal.[1] The exclusively male Farmer's Club held elaborate dinners at the members' houses, serving food supposedly grown (or shot) at their various estates. The wife of the host was expected to greet the men, and then retire gracefully as soon as dinner was announced.

This was enough activity for my father, outside of their usual social life with friends, although they did occasionally play a round of golf at the Sunnybrook Club. They never ate there, and I never went there at all; we had private tennis les-

---

1.    For 1 1/2 gallons: 1 1/2 cups sugar; 1 qt. fresh lemon juice; 2 qts. 100 proof Jamaican rum; 2 qts. cold water; 4 oz. peach brandy; 1 qt. cognac; 1 block of ice; 1 cup sliced fresh peaches.

sons at the Cadwaladers' court from a fat instructor called Mr. Bovee, and always swam at our grandparents' pool, or my Uncle Morris Cheston's in nearby Ambler.

My mother and father were religious, in a simple non-dogmatic way, and faithfully attended Sunday services at St. Thomas's Church, Whitemarsh. We children had to go too, and were often afflicted with pew-shaking "church giggles," especially when such things as "Mary's womb" were mentioned. Mummy and Aunt Mae always came to church with a supply of peppermint LifeSavers, which controlled us better than the fierce glares from Daddy while we squirmed through the long intellectual sermons preached by our Episcopal minister, Dr. Groton.

In my early years, table manners were constantly emphasized and corrected. Dinner with grownups meant sitting up straight, not letting your spine touch the back of the chair, and never putting elbows on the table. There was constant emphasis on cleaning up your plate, accompanied by lectures about the starving Armenians, although every child believed that even starving Armenians wouldn't eat over-cooked liver and fishy smelling flounder.

If the starving refugees came to our house, they might have been served vegetable water, a horrible dark green liquid that spinach or other greens had been boiled in. This was before the world publicized vitamins, anti-oxidants and carbohydrates, yet Margaret and the cook were already firm believers in this broth, as well as the benefits of cod liver oil, and plenty of milk and vegetables. Strangely, we almost never had salad in those days, and I never tasted garlic or pasta until I was married.

There were no frozen foods at all, except for ice cream, and that was homemade, from sugar, farm eggs and cream, plus fruit in season. The mixture was poured into a metal cylinder surrounded by chopped ice, set into a wooden barrel, and churned on the back porch every Sunday by Dominick, our kindly Italian gardener.

After church, like all children, I loved to help turn the crank of the ice-cream freezer, and afterwards lick the ice cream off the paddle. My favorite kinds were fresh peach, and a delicate caramel…topped with thin caramel syrup and crunchy caramelized spun sugar.

Sunday lunch was always the same: a standing rib roast cooked rare, Yorkshire pudding, roast potatoes, a green vegetable, and that sublime ice cream. It was followed by the obligatory walk through the fields with my father. When we came home, he would turn on the tall wooden Philco radio, which was hidden behind a screen in the living room, and tune in to what was left of the afternoon symphony. With the orchestra in full flight, he would fall sound asleep on the sofa, the Sunday paper spread open across his stomach, and I thankfully escaped to my room.

# 4

## *My Upstairs Downstairs Life*

We called the servants' wing the "Back Hall." There was nothing derogatory about the term. We were expected to treat everyone who worked for us with the same courtesy and thoughtfulness we would show our relatives, or royalty for that matter, in the unlikely event we should ever meet any. Orders were given only by adults, and were phrased semi-apologetically: "I'm sorry to bother you, but would you mind…" When my mother was downstairs and needed something from the pantry, she seldom rang the bell, but went and fetched it herself, and rinsed the glass or dish afterwards.

Winnie Brogan was my mother's right hand for all the forty-five years of her service. She had thick black hair turning a bit grey; steel rimmed glasses, strong smiling features, a substantial motherly bosom, and a hearty Irish brogue. She comforted the homesick, kept the young Irish maids in line, and trained the new-comers. Besides being the trusted keeper of the silver, she was the one who mixed and served the cocktails, and doled out the cookies—ladyfingers, Petit Beurres, Sweet Maries and homemade Sand Tarts (sugar cookies topped by a single blanched almond), which she kept in a special closet along with a huge tin of salty, crunchy Pennsylvania Dutch pretzels.

Delia Lavin, the parlor maid and Winnie's helper, was much younger. Her duties were caring for the downstairs rooms, setting the table, carrying the tea things and answering the front doorbell. Delia was a pretty, fresh-faced Irish girl and rumored to have an actual boyfriend. This turned out to be true when she left us during the war to get married and work in a beauty parlor.

Because the maids had so little time off, it was almost impossible for them to find boyfriends…and Winnie kept close tabs on the men servants to make sure they didn't take liberties. However, Jenny, Mummy's lady's maid, was abruptly let go, with no explanations to me. I missed her greatly, but was given no reasons for her sudden absence. Years later I learned that it was on account of a pregnancy, all the more shocking because her seducer was Tommy Dunn, our charming and cheerful second chauffeur. He was kept on in spite of his indiscretion, evidence of the sexual double standard of the times. Looking back on that episode, I can only hope that Jenny was taken care of somehow, in some forgiving place.

When I was a little girl, I spent much of my spare time in the back hall with my friends the maids, baking cakes from scratch or concocting savory leftovers for the dogs, while our bad-tempered cook Annie had her nap. (There were no cake mixes or canned dog food in those days.) The cakes usually turned out pretty flat, because I couldn't resist opening the heavy oven door to check on them every ten minutes, testing with a straw plucked from the kitchen broom. The straws must have been dirty, but concerns about sanitation didn't seem to bother us. However, those early experiments started me off on a lifelong love of cooking.

I also loved hanging around in the garage learning to use hammers and screwdrivers, and helping the chauffeurs wash the cars with gobs of soft amber-colored soap, the kind that came in big wooden barrels. After we soaped up the cars we hosed them down, and dried them with supple, slippery chamois cloths. It was fun turning the wheel on the big grindstone while Tommy sharpened the axes, trying to catch bright showers of cool sparks. I learned basic carpentry skills from the men, and always enjoyed trying to fix things. I had good lessons in patience when I took something apart, like my radio, and after "fixing it" discovered a leftover piece that wouldn't fit back in. Then Tommy made me do everything all over again, more methodically.

Margaret always gave me the same advice: "If at first you don't succeed, try, try again." This lesson was drawn from her tale about Robert the Bruce, a Scottish Chieftain, who was hiding out in a cave, discouraged about his many defeats by the British. Despondently, he watched a spider, trying and failing repeatedly to spin a thin strand of web over the entrance to the cave. Finally, after numerous attempts, she made the connection. Perseverance! Success!

Happy times were spent sitting at the controls of our old Ford V8 pickup truck, working the throttle and choke levers attached to the steering wheel, and honking the horn, which made a splendid hoarse "AOOOGAH!" noise. The engine started with a hand crank, and I was always warned to stand well back because someone had gotten in the way once, and the crank flew around and broke his arm.

The men were patient and kind, full of jokes and teasing stories. Dear old George Burns, the head chauffeur and former coachman had a bit of a drinking problem, which I didn't understand at my innocent age. I just thought he walked funny sometimes, and smelled strange. He drove my parents out to dinner in the big town car, a sleek black Cadillac, which had a specially built Brewster body. The dove-gray upholstery stank of exhaust fumes, and made me woozy whenever

I rode in it. Carbon monoxide fumes used to seep inside, and we children always got horribly carsick on long trips. This opulent car embarrassed my mother, who disliked any form of showing off.

She often told me that she wished the addition that they put on the house, after she and Daddy married to accommodate the enlarged family, wasn't so large. (The dining room was huge, had gilt moldings, and a table that could extend to seat twenty-four.) Mummy thought it ostentatious, and she would have preferred to live on a real farm, with cackling hens, a few cows and horses, and a cozy little house. But she was a captive of the Drexel tradition of grand houses, and she made the best of it with her own modest and cheerful nature. It was Daddy who loved the trappings of wealth, and he was quite a snob in spite of his practical hardworking nature.

When going out to winter dinners, Mummy and Daddy sat in the back of the Cadillac bundled under a fur rug. Between the front and back seat was a window that cranked up and down. They could talk to "Burns," as they called him, through a funnel-shaped mouthpiece on a flexible chrome speaking tube. The driver's seat was on the outside of the car, with no roof and no protection except the windscreen. It had a canvas top, which could be snapped into place with great difficulty in case of rain or snow.

On formal occasions, Burns wore a snappy black cap with a shiny visor, britches, buttoned up jacket, black leather puttees, and an ordinary black wool overcoat. Once he had a horribly infected toe, and much to my father's disapproval, he cut the front out of a black overshoe, and drove with his bare toes exposed.

A few nips must have been a great solace when he socialized in the help's dining room with the other chauffeurs and servants during the dinners where my parents were guests. No doubt all of them finished up quite an assortment of drinks and leftovers and had a jolly time of it, gossiping about their employers, before the long cold drive home with Mummy and Daddy snoozing in the furry luxury of the back seat.

Tommy Dunn always drove me to and from school. I adored him, and I followed him about constantly, while he kept up a patter of teasing jokes in his thick Scottish accent. He built me a beautifully crafted tree house, in an old gnarled apple tree, just like a real little house with a shingle roof, and windows that opened. It had a trap door with a secret latch, and a ladder you could pull up to keep out grownups, as well as those unlucky children who weren't allowed in our Cousins' Club. I "helped" him every chance I had, and spent long hours up there, imagining in my Tarzan daydreams that I was in the topmost branches of a jungle rainforest. I used to swing down on a rope, leap onto the back of my poor stuffed donkey, and stab him with a wooden dagger until his sawdust ran out. I wasn't very ladylike!

Later when I was grown and married, I visited the old family place and discovered that the tree house had been only about 15 feet off the ground. Still it was a wonderful place to hide, dream and read, and to escape when I felt sad.

I loved climbing trees, and fearlessly imitated my hero, Tarzan. Once when I was about eight, my mother called me downstairs from the third floor nursery to introduce me to some British relatives, the Countess of Winchelsea and her son, Christopher Finch-Hatten (cousin of Denys, the big game hunter and lover of *Out of Africa* writer Isak Dinesen).

I had just "fashioned" (I often thought in Edgar Rice Burroughs language) a loincloth by pinning two washcloths together, and I remember swinging topless down the three flights of stairs, Tarzan-style, twirling around the newel posts, beating my chest and giving the yodeling cry of the bull ape, landing in my ape crouch in the middle of the tea party. My mother was mortified, but the proper British guests were too polite to question what sort of a strange little daughter my family kept in the attic!

In reality, they probably enjoyed me. They were humorous and adventurous Brits. The Countess, Cousin Margaretta (Drexel) later became the leader of Britain's Woman's Land Army; her son, Christopher bravely helped ferry soldiers back from Dunkirk, and his sister Henrietta became a motorcycle dispatch rider.

Playing in the ground floor of the two-story garage was all right with my family, but I felt instinctively there was something mysterious and scary about the rooms in back of the garage where the men lived, because they forbade me ever to go there. I never knew why, exactly, until once I ventured into the chauffeurs' sitting room: a dark place, with a big sofa covered in greasy striped canvas. On the sofa was a newspaper with pink pages, called *The Police Gazette.* When I opened it, I saw photographs of women dressed in high boots, corsets, garter belts, stockings…and nothing else. I left in a hurry. I never confessed to breaking the rules, and never dared to go back.

Every morning before breakfast with Daddy, I would go into the maids' dining room—a big room off the kitchen—to say good morning. All the maids sat at one long table, covered with a different linen cloth each day, Winnie at one end and the two chauffeurs at the other.

They would admire my dress, and fuss over me and tell me to do well at school, and be good, and give me my favorite treat, the neatly decapitated tops off their boiled eggs. I loved them all, with their soft brogues, kind words, and jolly laughter. I never heard angry words among the maids, although there must have been some terrible fights and jealousies among so many women.

I remember only two who were not so nice. Annie the cook was one. She had a dreadful temper, and would slam down the sizzling iron frying pans, her wispy grey hair flying, her stockings rolled below her knobby knees, yelling at the terrified, overworked young kitchen maids. It was no wonder she was bad-tempered. In those days before prepared foods, Annie had to cook early breakfast at seven a.m. for the staff, then breakfast for the family at eight, then a big sit-down lunch at noon (called "dinner") for the staff, followed by a three-course lunch for my mother and any guests at one, then tea for the family, and supper (called "tea") for the staff at five-thirty.

Finally, after all that, at seven-thirty, she cooked a formal dinner of three courses for the family, plus an earlier supper for me on a tray, carried up by Margaret and set on a table in front of my radio. Until I was ten years old, I didn't eat meals with the family, except breakfast and sometimes on weekends when there weren't guests. In Philadelphia, "the family" meant one's mother and father. No one used the word "parents."

The other servant who was not so nice was the lady's maid, Mummy's replacement for the unfortunate Jenny. This was tall, dour Eleanor Boyd, an outsider in our servant quarters because she was a Northern Irish Protestant among the warm-hearted Irish Catholics. She gave herself airs on account of being Madame's personal maid. Eleanor had no sense of humor, and she wouldn't let me work her Singer sewing machine. Her predecessor Jenny had patiently taught me to sew, and I enjoyed piecing scraps of material together, pumping away madly on the treadle that ran the machine.

No one liked Eleanor much, but she was a talented seamstress, and she kept my mother's Paris frocks and custom-made suits to perfection. My mother loved crisp tailored clothes; the same tailor who made her riding habits, P.N. Degerburg, made all her town and traveling suits.

It seemed to me that Mummy's hems were forever being altered up and down according to fashion's dictates. She spent long boring hours being fitted while Eleanor knelt on the bathroom floor, her mouth full of pins, making tiny adjustments.

I loved to watch her dress for a party, with Eleanor assisting like a nurse at an operation. First came the ugly pink corset, which she didn't need, but which women still wore in the 1930's. In front of the corset was the long stiff whalebone fastener, the "busk," with its two rows of tiny hooks that had to be painstakingly done up. A camisole type brassiere had to be fastened with more hooks in the back, then real silk sheer stockings fastened to the corset tabs and silk "drawers" with wide legs and a tiny button at the waist.

Then, Eleanor dipped a big swans-down powder puff into a crystal bowl filled with silky white Chanel #5 scented powder and dusted my mother's bare shoulders and back. Finally the long evening dress was eased over her head, snaps and hooks done up, combing jacket put on over the evening gown, hairdo adjusted, Chanel perfume dabbed on, jewelry selected and fastened, and a veil pinned into place to keep her hair from blowing on the car trip. Tiny satin high-heeled slippers had been selected in a color to match the frock.

A quick glance in the long mirror, for she was never vain, and she would pick up her brocaded or beaded evening purse, which Eleanor had packed with lipstick, compact, handkerchief, comb, gold cigarette case filled with Chesterfields, and two celluloid-tipped cigarette holders. All was completed just in time before the inevitable bellow from my father downstairs: "Hurry up, Frances! We're going to be late."

My mother went to Jean the hairdresser in Chestnut Hill, about once a week, and had her lovely oblong nails manicured twice a month. The style then was French fashion, with half moons showing, and the polish palest pink. She loved picking up local gossip from Jean and his helpers. I remember her announcing to my father at the dinner table, "They say the Allies' invasion of France will be next week." "Just WHO says?" asked my father crossly. "It is only the best kept secret in the whole world." "Jean the Hairdresser," answered my mother smugly. Jean turned out to be 100% correct; it did happen the next week: June 6, 1944.

In those days hair was curled by means of a fiendish permanent-wave machine fastened to the ceiling. Long snakes ending in curling rods descended from the heating element, and the hair was rolled onto the hot curlers. This usually resulted in frizz, and then to make things worse, the hair for elderly, grey-haired ladies was tinted an alarming blue.

Teatime in the back hall was even more fun than breakfast. There were delicious scones, raisin soda bread, and boiling hot black tea in thick white porcelain cups. The maids (often called "the Girls") tipped their tea into the saucers and blew to cool it: a sensible solution, I thought, although I wasn't allowed to do it if I had tea in the big living room.

Our tea trays were formal. A little alcohol burner sat under the silver kettle to keep the water hot, and the cups and teapot were of delicate flowered china. Even the tea itself was different: Chinese Hu Kwa, smoky and pale. The lumps of sugar were dropped in the cups with silver tongs, and then one had a choice of thin slices of lemon, or thick yellow farm cream. Cinnamon sugar was spread on buttery toast triangles, kept warm under a china dome, and usually tiny sponge cupcakes or ladyfingers were arranged on silver trays set on a three-tiered mahogany cake stand. In the winter, if there were no guests, the tea was sometimes served in Mummy's bedroom in front of the fireplace.

She would be on the chaise lounge, wearing one of her lovely long tea gowns, and it was another special treat for me to be there with her, even though the tea tasted funny, and I missed my time in the servants' dining room where they would swish the black tea leaves around in the bottom of the cup and tell my fortune.

The leaves made designs like Chinese calligraphy when they stuck to the side of the cup. I peered excitedly over the shoulder of whichever Irish maid specialized in reading and interpreting. "See there now, Frances! You're going to get a letter…or is it a big package, or a handsome visitor, or a new pet? And there's a number—what is it?" Turning the cup around on its side to read the number, she continues, "It looks like…a…95. Och, now, would that be the great mark you'll be getting on that spelling test tomorrow?"

Because my mother and father were so often away, that big house and its household were my whole world, and endlessly interesting. I especially loved the spicy-smelling cedar closet in the big attic. There were tall Louis Vuitton steamer trunks, fitted inside with drawers and hangers, plastered with colorful stickers announcing "Cunard Lines" or the names of ocean liners like *Europa* or *Mauritania*, or the warning "Not Wanted on Voyage," because the passenger had no need to use the contents until after the crossing.

The winter clothes in the attic closet were sorted and hung neatly on long poles if it was summertime, and summer clothes were hung up in the winter. Big stiff-sided cardboard boxes from fancy stores like Henri Bendel or Worth of Paris were stacked along the walls. These were packed with clothes no longer in fashion, neatly folded between layers and layers of tissue paper, and sprinkled with mothballs.

I was fascinated by the boxes of beautiful ivory fans, some from Paris, London, or Vienna, some with ostrich feathers or lace, and painted ones from China. My cousin and I snapped them open and peered over the top in a manner we thought to be coquettish while pretending to be ladies of the Court. On rainy days, when my school friends came over, we often chose dress-up clothes from a big wicker trunk full of costumes. There were long sequined evening dresses, and others of satin and chiffon, beaded and short, from the flapper days of the Roaring Twenties; ball gowns and brocade wraps from the turn of the century, Swiss dirndls, black satin bathing suits with wide Irish lace collars, Chinese robes, and the harlequin-patterned Pierrot and Pierrette costumes from the fancy-dress parties of the twenties and thirties that were much in vogue. There was even a fur cape—rabbit I guess, but we thought of it as ermine—and a rhinestone tiara to go with it.

This evening wrap ended up in our costume trunk
Bonne Mama

We loved dressing up, and I have kept the same trunk with many of these old clothes, hoping that my granddaughter and her friends might like to play-act, wobbling around in high-heeled satin slippers, pretending to be glamorous movie stars, or ladies of bygone days. Alas for modern children, television and video games have mostly replaced that sort of make-believe.

Another favorite place for me to hang out was the pantry, especially when I was allowed to turn the handle of the big wooden wheel, which made a delightful grinding noise when it sharpened the steel blades of our silver dinner knives, fitted into slots in the wheel.

The family didn't entertain very often. But when they did put on a formal dinner party, it was on a grand scale. The entire household went into bustling overdrive, with extra furniture polishing, cooking, and cleaning. In the spring and summer, my mother and Winnie fixed the baskets of flowers that George Schumm brought in almost every day. They arranged them in informal country style in big Chinese porcelain bowls (Famille Vert, and Famille Rose patterns) and placed them on the shining mahogany tables in the living rooms and library. I was no help at this job. My flowers always toppled over and I had to start over again in a bad temper. (PATIENCE!)

The blinds would be drawn against the midday heat, and the rooms smelled wonderfully of peonies, roses, and lilies. The furniture wore smart summer slipcovers of white linen, and the winter carpets were replaced with braided reed mats, everything perfectly set up to receive the guests.

In the pantry, Winnie carefully clicked the mysterious numbered dial of the big iron safe, clockwise and counterclockwise, just so. It was almost big enough for me to squeeze inside. The heavy door swung open to reveal the precious silver in yellow flannel bags labeled Tiffany, or JE Caldwell. I loved to help unwrap the vases and extra ornaments for the table, and sometimes I helped Winnie polish the silver. These rituals made everything feel like Christmas. It took two men to stretch the table to its full length, and to fit the heavy leaves in place. Then, the long, white damask cloth was draped so that it just cleared the floor, and a gleaming array of silver flower bowls, candlesticks, epergnes filled with nuts and candies, and a lovely procession of French bisque (porcelain) figurines was arranged down the center.

Each place setting had a cut-glass water tumbler, two or three delicate wine glasses—far smaller than today's—and gigantic monogrammed damask napkins, almost big enough to cover a bridge table. After these dinners, I noticed the red wine stains, and the lipstick kisses on those outsized napkins, and I felt sorry for the laundress. Lipstick in those days was almost indelible, especially "Tangee," which looked orange on the stick but turned blood red on the lips.

Cousin Julia Henry always made the "Best Dressed" list.
Her clothes were made in Paris, and her plaid bicycle seat was
custom-made to match her pedal-pushers.

I was usually made to come down and be introduced, or greet the guests, awkward and shy in my pajamas and tan Yeager (flannel) wrapper. My mother's cousin Julia Biddle Henry—a grand dame of Philadelphia society, reed-thin, bedecked with huge jewels, and blue hair done up in a puffy arrangement—made me feel the worst. "Don't you look sweet, little Frances? You are my godchild, you know!" She looked me critically up and down while I squirmed with embarrassment. I knew that I looked far from sweet, with my teeth in metal bands, and my square sturdy figure. And as for cousin Julia being a good godmother, the only present I ever received from her was a stuck-up porcelain French poodle with scratchy gray "fur," and I loathed it. I suspect that it was an unwanted ornament that someone else had given to her, and she just wrapped it up and brought it along as an afterthought. Once she pointed to one of her flashy jeweled pins—a giant topaz—and cooed, "This will be yours someday, Darling," but typically, that never happened.

My father always complained when he had to go to one of her dinners. He disliked her French cuisine and all the folderol connected with French wine. Ancient, threadbare chintz and tattered brocade covered her antique furniture. Clouds of dust and feathers puffed out when anyone sat down, which gave Daddy uncontrolled fits of sneezing and wheezing because of his allergies. He thought her eccentric, selfish and miserly, and mean to her henpecked husband, a lovely man. This was a curious anomaly for someone perennially on the "Best Dressed List" who bought her wardrobe in Paris each season.

I never liked my mother's oldest sister Aunt Minnie Cassatt, either. She usually wore black clothes and many diamonds, powdered her face flour-white, had pouting, purple-painted lips, and a discontented disposition. She didn't get along with my mother, who was far more intelligent and popular and who had apparently stolen her beaux with embarrassing ease when they were young. Aunt Minnie disliked me too. She preferred my cousin Minnie Cadwalader, who was her namesake and goddaughter.

(Years later, when I became engaged to Whitney Tower, I went to show off my lovely diamond engagement ring to Aunt Mae. When I reached her house, Aunt Minnie happened to be visiting. My cousin Minnie hadn't gotten engaged yet, and Aunt Minnie was displeased that I had attained this exalted status ahead of her goddaughter, and to a WHITNEY no less! Without acknowledging me, she unsnapped her ubiquitous black satin purse, stuffed with paper money. She shoved this into Minnie's hands, as some sort of weird compensation for not being the first niece to snag a husband. Later, my cousin and I had a good laugh, and she insisted we split the loot: twenty-three dollars each!)

I remember the grownups' parties: the rooms filled with pink-faced men, who smelled damply of whiskey and hair tonic, and who greeted me with jovial hugs and silly flirtatious questions. Almost all of my family's best friends were friendly and kind to me, like Mr. Mahlon Kline, who everyone affectionately called "Kliney"—a gentle, balding bachelor (founder of the pharmaceutical firm Smith Kline and French), and Mr. George Widener, a tall, silver-haired, courtly man who owned many great thoroughbred racehorses, and Mr. Sturgis Ingersoll, a knowledgeable art collector, and president of the Philadelphia Museum of Art. He had twinkling eyes, and a small black moustache waxed into needle sharp points. I used to wonder how he could safely kiss his wife without puncturing her.

I had favorites among the ladies, especially perky Mrs. Owen Toland, who was a fanatic fox hunter, and jolly, mannish Mrs. Marianna Coleman. My mother's best friend was "Stokesie"—Mrs. Louis Clark—so good-looking and full of fun. They all had a natural way of laughing and joking, making a young girl feel at ease. Mrs. Clark, later Mrs. Harold Weeks, was the mother of my first friend of the opposite sex, David Clark. In those days mothers and fathers always tried to promote friendships with children whose parents they knew, and were suspicious of others without appropriate pedigree.

Often the guests were family. I always loved my father's four jolly brothers—the Cheston Uncles: Charlie, Morris, Jimmy and Calvert. Uncle Morris, a distinguished lawyer, took on trusteeships for his many nieces and nephews, working selflessly and wisely on their behalf, without compensation, until his death. Their wives, my aunts, were interesting, modest and forthright.

Their unmarried sister, religious, straight-laced Aunt Lily Cheston was quite formidable for a young person, but later I knew her to have a warm and loving heart. The other sister, Aunt Charlotte, was seldom around, and I wish I had known her better. She was married to a Canadian doctor-missionary, Herman Moret. They lived in Labrador, diligently working all of their lives with Dr. Wilfred Grenfell in his Inuit mission.

Compared to that Upstairs world, the laundry room was an alien planet. A row of gray soapstone tubs was arrayed against one wall, each with its own corrugated tin washboard, and a wringer that squeezed water from the wet clothes when you turned the handle, as you fed them between its rubber rollers. A tall cylindrical coal stove stood in the center of the room, and there was a huge padded table with a mangle for ironing the sheets, napkins and tablecloths, and smaller tapered ironing boards for dresses and shirts. The laundry's steamy atmosphere was unbearable in summer.

For some reason, our laundresses were always Scandinavian or Middle European. I felt sorry for them; they seemed sad, and couldn't communicate with our Irish maids. They were considered "foreigners" because of the language barrier. The laundress finished ironing the sheets on those great padded tables, thumping down the heavy flat irons, which were heated on the coal-burning stove, replacing them as they cooled, testing the heat with a sizzle of a spit-moistened fingertip.

The irons came in graduated sizes, and rested in several rows on rims that circled the tapered stove; the smallest at the top for ruffles and lace, then larger ones for dresses, and finally the biggest irons for sheets, tablecloths, blankets and towels. The coal fire had to be kept going at just the right temperature; heating the irons so they pressed properly without burning the delicate linens and silks was a difficult art. It must have been a monumental task to take care of the household's washing, all done by hand.

No wonder none of the laundresses stayed very long. I especially remember Marta. She let me wash Duggie in her big tub, and laughed at the way he changed from a black furry Scottie pup to a miserable soaking wet rat. I tried to help sometimes, and I turned the crank of the wringer for her. Her hands were red and wrinkled from hours in the hot soapy water.

I was never fully aware of the personal unhappiness, which probably lay behind the smiling kindly faces of the servants in "the Back." How homesick they must have been, so far away from their mothers and fathers and families across the wide ocean. They never spoke of the past, at least not to my parents or me, and I wish I had asked more questions about their early lives.

My mother hated the rituals of hiring new help. I remember her distress on the phone, talking to the mean-spirited, avaricious woman in charge of a mysterious place called the Intelligence Office, explaining the vacant position. They would then arrange an appointment in town for the dreaded interview, dreaded by both the prospective maid and my kind-hearted mother. She always saw the good side of anyone, and if the prospective maid had even a marginally positive reference from a house comparable to ours, Mummy would hire her. I believe she would have hired an Irish hatchet-murderess if the woman's face and brogue were appealing.

The great advantage of being the daughter in such a big household was the feeling of security and love. I was insulated from any unpleasant reality, and the bigger world never showed me its ugly or challenging face. I wasn't even aware of the Great Depression, yet there I was growing up in the middle of it, in oblivious luxury. I know that it concerned my parents at the time, because they took care of—and felt responsible for—many retired retainers. Servants who had cared for my grandparents were now sustained on pensions from my parents. My mother and father visited these retired servants often, showed them many kindnesses, and eventually attended their funerals.

I remember my mother remarking, as she signed a monthly check for a faithful member of her own mother's household: "Marie Hansen! She must be at least one hundred years old!"

Government social programs weren't in place yet, except for the National Recovery Act (NRA) and the Civilian Conservation Corps (CCC), which were just getting under way. There was a low income tax, no capital gains tax, and President Roosevelt's New Deal wasn't established yet.

My family and most of their circle despised FDR and all forms of government interference, especially that utmost abomination: the federal income tax. To my parents, "That Man in the White House" was a "Traitor to his Class," and Eleanor Roosevelt was a "meddlesome left-winger."

In those days household help often spent their entire working lives in the service of one family, forty or fifty years sometimes, and then counted on their employers to see them through their old age...there being no Social Security, or government welfare programs. They were considered part of the family. In general, many people of that era were too proud to accept unearned handouts. The accepted ethic was hard work and plenty of it. But then came the Depression, and even the most resolute couldn't find employment.

My family provided hot lunches for the poor, twice a week. We followed the example set long ago by my great-grandparents, the Anthony Drexels. In our case, the poor were a shifting colony of itinerant men, who camped in a "Hooverville" (or "Hobo Jungle") near the Reading Railroad tracks, a few miles from our house.

On set days of the week, three or four shabby men wearing mismatched suits made their way across the fields from their shanty towns along the tracks, showing up in time for lunch on our back kitchen porch. I liked sitting with them and watching while they stuffed themselves on heaping plates of Irish stew, mopping up the gravy with slices of Wonder Bread, and devouring large slabs of pie washed down with steaming cups of strong hot tea or coffee. I perched on the big garbage bin and listened to their tales, laughing at their jokes and snatches of song. They treated me kindly, and a high spot came when one of them taught me how to spit through the gap in my front teeth. Another tried in vain to teach me how to whistle by sticking my thumb and forefinger against my teeth. He sounded like a siren when he did it, but all I ever managed was a spitty sort of hooting.

Another homeless man played jolly tunes on his harmonica, and he said he'd teach me next time if I got my own. I was longing to learn. I begged until my mother finally bought me a Hohner Marine Band harmonica, but all I could ever produce was a painful series of in and out wheezes, and sadly, my promised music teacher never returned for the lesson.

We called these victims of the Depression "tramps," although we never used this word in their presence. They were invariably polite and grateful, and everyone in our household liked them. There was never a hint that they might be potential thieves or drunkards, or unfit companions for a child.

The only time I remember Margaret being worried about these visitors was one evening on our way back from the Cadwaladers, when we were taking a new shortcut through the pinewoods at the top of our hill. We came upon a campsite, with a little pup tent, and a burnt place where there had been a recent campfire. Scattered about were dirty old clothes and empty pint bottles with whiskey labels. I was intrigued, and wanted to crawl into the tent, but Margaret hustled me away as fast as she could. She was scared, but I didn't understand why.

Something changed suddenly in March 1932, when I was five, and from that point on, my cousins and I were kept even more strictly under someone's watchful eye. I was too young to have read the newspaper headlines about the Lindbergh baby's kidnapping, but I overheard the servants' dramatic recounting of the details as they sipped their afternoon tea. White wooden bars were suddenly installed outside the windows of the third-floor nursery, although I thought it unlikely that a kidnapper would carry a thirty-foot ladder just to get at me. The awful discovery of the Lindbergh baby's body in the woods, two months later in mid-May, is vivid in my memory. I remember wondering if the birds had covered him with leaves, like the story of the two little Babes in the Woods. The fairy tales of my childhood melded with real life sometimes.

Our servants loved scandals and gossip. The more lurid the crimes, the more exaggerated the story became with each discussion. "Och! The monster, Hauptmann, that horrible Hun! And that puir wee innocent child and the lovely family!"

Much later, the events of 1939 intruded on our lives. I wondered why my father had not come down at the usual time for his breakfast, and I ran upstairs to say good morning. I saw my parents uncharacteristically sitting together on my father's bed. They had been listening to the radio, and my mother was crying. "What's wrong? Don't be sad," I said, frightened by their seriousness. "Hitler has invaded Poland," Daddy told me. "This will mean war." His voice gave me a chill that I remember to this day.

The war did come, someplace far away in Europe, but I was safe on the third floor, innocent in my sheltered security, until September of 1940 when I was sent to Foxcroft, a boarding school in Virginia. I was fourteen. My faithful, patient and loving Margaret stayed with us until I went away.

Later, I learned that the family had often discussed "letting her go," and hiring a more cultured French governess to supervise me. I might have learned French, it is true, but I would have been separated from my second mother, and it would have broken my heart.

# 5

## *My Two Mothers*

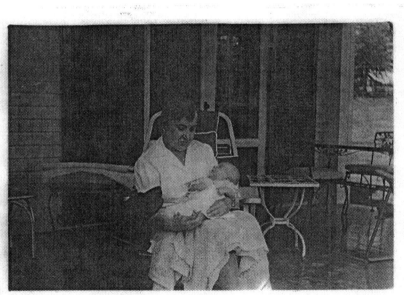

1951 — Margaret and our oldest son Whitney Tower, Jr.

Margaret Carney Smith was born in a grim stone cottage in the little fishing village of New Haven on the Firth of Forth, just north of Edinburgh, Scotland. She arrived at our house in 1929 when I was three years old to be my nurse—we didn't call them "nannies" then—and she stayed for eleven years, until I left for boarding school. When I unpacked my trunk that first confusing night away at school, I sobbed homesick tears over every piece of clothing that she had packed with such loving care. Dearest Marg, humorous, loyal, and loving: my constant, watchful companion; my second mother.

She was strong and compactly built, always dressed in a starched white uniform, her sturdy legs encased in brown lisle or white cotton stockings. Bunions stretched her large black oxfords into peculiar shapes and her kind hands were large and careworn.

Her hair remained black for almost all of her life, but she bemoaned its lack of natural curl, and her main complaint about me was my own straight hair. She spent many futile minutes trying to coax a "wee wave" into my limp mousy locks.

I despised hearing about her previous charge, the impossibly obedient Jacqueline, the one with the curly golden head of hair. "Och, what a gorgeous wee child," she used to say, "a wee doll!" Yuck, I thought, I bet she plays with dolls and never climbs trees!

Margaret used to read to me endlessly and patiently, and never failed to come to my bedside to chase away my nightmares, to hold my hot little head when I was sick, to stay up with me when I had to get up to go to the bathroom in the night.

It was a cruel thing, that final parting from Margaret, in the fall of 1940. This separation ended her employment by my family, and she had to go to California, hired by my sister to take care of her young daughter. But there was a happy ending. I married in 1947, and Margaret came back two years later to be the nurse for my own first-born daughter. Margaret was ageless, wise, and infinitely patient. I loved her dearly, and missed her long after I grew up.

She had a great sense of humor, a broad Scots accent, and loved gossip and intrigue. Sweaters, socks, mittens and scarves reeled off her clicking knitting needles. Most of the time she shrugged off my brother George's fiendish practical jokes, and she hardly ever complained about him to my parents. One of the few times she was really hurt and humiliated was when he found an advertisement for Dr. Scholl's corn plasters and bunion pads. George succeeded somehow in persuading Dr. Scholl himself to drive all the way from his office in Germantown to our house in Oreland for a private consultation with "Miss Smith." Marg certainly did have bunions, and she was embarrassed about them.

The doctor rang the doorbell, and Delia was dispatched to fetch "Miss Smith." I still remember her chagrin and the doctor's anger, when Margaret, in her white nurse's uniform, had to confess she hadn't ordered the visit, had no money, and she was merely the child's nurse in this imposing house. The doctor roared off, gravel spattering from beneath the wheels of his black Model T, which had **DR. SCHOLL'S CORN PLASTERS** printed on the door in large yellow letters.

George was labeled a "limb of Satan" by the help, and he never stopped teasing them. One snowy afternoon, he talked the younger ones—Margaret, Peggy, Jenny, Katie the kitchen maid, and two of the Cadwaladers' more susceptible maids—into climbing up the steep Cadwalader hill to the very top, where he had rigged up our long four-person Flexible Flyer with two smaller sleds roped on behind. Why the servants obeyed George that day I have no idea...except that he was very persuasive, and the outing might have represented an unusual adventure in their routine lives. He arranged the girls on the three sleds, the plumpest ones on the four-seater in the front, and he showed them how to prop their feet up on the foot rests, and work the steering bar.

The victims wore their cotton uniforms, flimsy underwear, lisle stockings, unbuckled flapping galoshes, and long tweed coats. No one wore long pants in those days, and when George pushed off the sled-loads of girls down the icy slope, the cold wet snow sprayed up under their skirts. Everyone screamed, no one knew how to steer, and the lighter sleds veered and yawed. They tangled in the ropes, crashed into the big sled, and all six girls fell off in a shrieking melee of waving legs and arms. There was some blood, lots of bruises, icy thighs and faces, and our two families were furious with him. After much soothing and reassuring by my mother and Aunt Mae, none of them quit, and George was made to apologize to each one of them individually.

I think of Margaret as my second mother. It was Marg who watched over me for all the everyday chores, made me do my homework, supervised my bath, accompanied me to the dentist, watched me climb trees, taught me to knit and sew, told me tales of the "old country," got me fed and dressed for school, took me on long walks no matter what the weather, and sang wonderful songs and hymns in her rich contralto voice.

Because my parents were away for weeks at a time, staying at the South Carolina plantation, or the fox hunting farm in Unionville, or off on other sporty adventures like salmon fishing in Canada, or grouse shooting in Scotland, the best times for me were when Mummy was home, a special treat. She was the delicious smelling apparition who climbed the three flights of stairs to kiss me good night, who was always great fun to talk to and a cozy, sympathetic listener.

Spending time with my mother was like savoring an exotic spun-sugar dessert after a routine meal. It was Mummy who took me on outings, away from the house. Margaret didn't drive.

Unlike my father who was cranky and lost his temper often, my mother had a sunny disposition. But if I was rude, or if I did something unkind or thoughtless, her instant disapproval and direct blue-eyed gaze were something to be reckoned with.

On humid summer days she might whisk me away in her shiny little Chevy convertible for a visit to the drugstore in Chestnut Hill or some other errand, allowing me to ride in the exciting, blowy rumble seat with the breeze in my face.

The drugstore was called Whittem's after its proprietor, pharmacist Bill Whittem. His store had two huge glass jars inside the plate-glass front window—one filled with green liquid and the other with red, the traditional pharmacist's sign.

Mr. Whittem was a jolly, talkative man who prepared the prescriptions himself, choosing different powders from the hundreds of ceramic jars and glass bottles on the shelves, and mashing them up with mortar and pestle. All the labels were in Latin, handwritten in bold black italic script. He also mixed a special curry powder, which gave the store its own exotic spicy smell. Next door was an ice cream parlor, and a scoop of homemade French vanilla in its brown, crisp sugar cone was the perfect treat for a hot summer's day.

Mummy and I shared a passion for hot dogs, which my father despised. If he happened to drive us into Chestnut Hill, he would sit in the car fuming, while Mummy and I indulged in our vice. "You'll ruin your stomachs," he'd say. "God only knows what they put in those things." Mummy thought he was jealous because his ulcer wouldn't let him eat wieners.

Another favorite outing with my mother was the trip up to Camp Hill to my grandparents' house for a swim in their pool. If we went swimming right after the pool was filled—with icy water, straight from an artesian well—this was less of a swim and more like a gasping, shocking dunk among Arctic floes. It was a beautiful pool, ten feet deep, with azure tiles from the edges to the bottom, and no shallow end. There weren't any filters in those days, and after a week or so the pool might be a little warmer, but green with algae, and we dog-paddled around in it among the resident frogs.

Many times my cousins would be there too. Ordered to "get out this minute!" we protested that our blue lips and uncontrolled shivering did not mean we were actually cold, and we begged for one last dip. Then, reluctantly, we changed in the dressing rooms that had last year's forgotten, bedraggled suits still drooping on the pegs. There were four cubicles for the men and four for the ladies, arranged around a raised terrace overlooking the swimmers. Finally evicted from the pool, we had great times exploring the extensive grounds, while Mummy and Aunt Mae swam round and round doing the breast stroke, wearing white rubber bathing caps, rubber bathing slippers that laced around their thin white ankles, and made-to-order "bathing costumes." These were always black, or navy, with long pleated knee-length skirts.

They both loved to laugh, and told funny gossipy stories in their deep voices, taking advantage of a quiet spell without having to dodge splashing cannonballs, and endless competitive attempts at fancy dives. They never ran out of conversation, even after talking for hours to each other on the phone every day.

When my father took one of his rare swims in the pool, I was embarrassed by his bathing suit: a white woolen undershirt, and navy wool shorts that reached almost to his knees, cinched around his considerable tummy with a white buckled belt. I thought him too fat for such an outfit.

Up the hill, behind Camp Hill Hall, there was a carriage house containing a sleigh and antique carriages and buggies that we could climb up into and bounce on, while pretending to escape from highwaymen, lashing our imaginary horses with the ancient buggy whips. There was also a strange stuffy little room up a twisting flight of stairs, where the groom used to sleep, but we never played there.

Next to the carriage house was an airless, long-abandoned and cobwebby squash court and close by, a big greenhouse. This was presided over by Hughie Murray, the bent-over, kindly gardener, who used to be our grandparents' head coachman. The humid greenhouse smelt deliciously of all the varieties of flowers grown there, and especially the heavy musky scent from plump Muscat grapes, hanging in shiny green bunches from an ancient vine, as big around as a twisted tree.

Hughie would beckon us into his walk-in ice room, cold and welcome after the heat in the glass house, and formally present each of the girls with miniature bouquets of sweetheart roses, all done up in paper lace doilies. Newly cut flowers were waiting in pails to be brought up to the house.

Racing back to the pool for the final "just one more" dip of the day, we intersected the procession of maids: usually three of them, wearing their best afternoon uniforms. They had to make their long way down from our grandparents' house over the lawn to the pool, balancing pitchers of iced tea, garnished with fresh mint, crystal glasses on silver trays, and carrying plates of tiny sandwiches, sponge cakes, ladyfingers, and the ice bucket with its silver tongs.

The head butler, an unbendingly dignified man named Priest, followed the procession. He wore his habitual uniform of morning coat and striped trousers, and was much too grand to do any of the carrying, saving his energy for pouring the iced tea.

If we were lucky we would meet up with Pollack, the night watchman. He was Irish, funny, and talkative, and he had the scary attraction of having a gleaming steel hook for a hand, like Peter Pan's notorious pirate Captain Hook.

In the early thirties my grandmother Sarah Van Rensselaer had died, and my grandfather, "Mr. Van," was living by himself in the big house, but with the same enormous staff to look after him. He was a kind good-natured gentleman, much beloved, with big mustaches and a deep rumbly voice. When grandchildren and their friends were swimming, he would come down to the pool at teatime to watch the fun.

He dressed formally, even in the warmest weather, in jacket, necktie and waistcoat with a droopy gold watch chain, and summer-weight white flannel trousers with grey pinstripes. He usually wore a mellow Panama hat, and always carried a gold or ivory-headed cane. He was a staunch Princeton supporter, a yachtsman, and a leader in civic affairs in Philadelphia, especially the Philadelphia Orchestra. After his beloved wife Sarah's death, he kept the black mourning band around his sleeve for many years.

My cousins and I always called my grandparents "Bum Mama and Bump Papa," because that was what I thought my mother and my aunts told us to call them. It was not until much later that I saw these names correctly written down, and then I realized that they were French: *Bonne Mama* and *Bon Papa*.

I was brought up by my family's Victorian example, which was never to admit to hurt feelings, physical pain, or sadness. If I fell off my bike, or crashed on roller skates, I tried not to cry when the stinging iodine was applied. "I'm fine" was the only acceptable response. (This attitude, like the exhortation to get right back up on the horse after being bucked off, and to "carry on" no matter what, is certainly different from the sharing of emotion, and the pill for every spectrum of complaint, which is today's way.)

A common Philadelphia attitude, which prevailed in those days, was the dearth of any physical affection or demonstrative love. This somehow implied weakness, or a need for attention, and there were very few hugs and kisses exchanged, even after long absences. Brothers and sisters shook hands, and a peck on the cheek for good night or good morning sufficed for parents, belying the deep affection we actually felt for one another.

I remember Margaret as the comforting one, with her hug and "puir wee thing," and welcomed her kindness. The chance for me to shed tears freely was almost like a secret between us.

My mother was the organizer of special events, but it was Margaret who really took constant responsibility in all matters that didn't involve driving a car. Every single day—rain or shine, snow, sleet, boiling hot—she insisted that we take a long walk that she called a "constitutional."

"Och, Frenzie." She had a thick Scottish burr, and that was how my name "Francie" came out. "Hurry along now, a wee walk will do ye good, and it will bring the roses into your cheeks." Nowadays, even in bad weather, my memories of Margaret make me feel guilty to stay indoors.

The walks were never boring, with my dog investigating every last enticing smell, and Marg singing the old music-hall songs like:

> *Abba dabber dabber dab said the monkey to the chimp.*
> *Abba dabber dabber dab said the chimpy to the monk*
> *Then the big baboon one night in June,*
> *He married them, and very soon*
> *They went upon their Abba Dabba Honeymoon!*

Another song that she loved to sing was "Who paid the rent for Mrs. Rip Van Winkle, when Rip Van Winkle was away?" She knew songs from the Boer War that she had learned from her brother in the British Army and often sang Gilbert and Sullivan. She loved the grand old hymns like "In the Garden" and "The Old Rugged Cross." She knew all of Sir Harry Lauder's songs, and she taught me to recite one even though I didn't understand all the words:

> *Just a wee deoch an dorris,*
> *Just a wee dram, that's a'…*
> *Just a wee deoch and Doris,*
> *Before we gang awa'…*
> *There's a wee wifie waitin'*
> *In a wee butt-and-ben,*
> *If you can say it's a braw bricht moonlicht nicht the nicht*
> *Then you're aw' richt, ye ken!*

She explained to me that a "butt-and-ben" was a two-room cottage in the Scottish highlands, but the rest of the song remained a mystery. I didn't realize until years later that being able to recite this song was a Scottish sobriety test, and the song is about whiskey. *"Deoch an dorris"* is Scots Gaelic for "open the door," so a wee deoch an dorris is the drink that's "one for the road."

Before immigrating to America at the age of twenty-five, Marg was a member of the fisherwomen's choir from her village of New Haven. She once sang at a command performance before Her Royal Highness Queen Mary. One of her proudest possessions was the photograph of the choir, taken on that great day, wearing their traditional costume of tucked-up striped petticoats, white woolen stockings, black shoes with silver buckles, and pointed Dutch style caps.

Marg was a great storyteller, and she loved to talk. The vivid tales of her childhood on the Firth of Forth thrilled me, especially the story about the "wee bairn" who, looking for shells at low tide against her mother's orders, rode her little tricycle away out onto the wide flat sands. The tide came sweeping in, and the little girl was drowned. The tricycle was found at next tide, evidence of what had happened.

This was a cautionary tale aimed at my chronic disobedience, and it made a lasting impression, especially the description of the sodden little body washed up many days later against the breakwater that guarded the harbor.

The print by Landseer that my family had at our plantation house always reminded me of this sad tale. It showed a half-drowned girl, lying on a dock, watched over by her rescuer, a great noble Saint Bernard.

Margaret's father was a sailor with the herring fleet, venturing far out into the treacherous and dangerous North Sea. If there had been a terrible storm, all the small children and the wives would go down to the pier, anxiously waiting for news of the boats, or the first sighting of a sail on the horizon. There was many a sad drowning from that village, and the poignant tales of bereavement affected me deeply, as I imagined myself as one of the little daughters, waiting for the Daddy who would never return from the sea.

The song that Margaret sang for me went like this: *"Seagull, seagull fly away over the sea. Tell my Daddy that his little Francie is waiting and praying for thee."* She would sing it to me on the dock at our house in Maine, and I was sure that the swooping gulls would deliver the message to my own father, working away in hot old Philadelphia.

Marg was deeply religious. Every Sunday night without fail, our chauffeur, Tommy Dunn, drove her to the big Presbyterian Church in Oreland. For these services she wore a silk dress and a shiny black straw hat that she had trimmed herself with paper flowers in the spring, or ribbon in the winter. When Margaret drove away, I was terribly worried that she wouldn't come back to me, even to the point of being sick to my stomach, and sobbing for her return. This baffled and angered my mother and father, who did their best to reassure me, without success. After all, they reasoned, they were my parents, and they couldn't understand why I was so distressed and anxious for the short time Marg was at church. I guess they didn't understand my deep need of her in my life.

Margaret often read to me from the moral lessons in a tattered volume called *Bible Stories in Pictures*, which contained vivid etchings of Lot's wife turning into a pillar of salt, Jonah being swallowed by the whale, and the crumbling house that had been built upon the sand. She taught me about Jesus and his love for little children.

I loved the story she told about Joseph and his coat of many colors. The reason, she explained, was that because of his family's poverty, it was patched with multiple scraps of cloth. Her poem went: "Jacob made his wee son Josey a tartan coat to keep him cosy."

Many of her maxims have stayed with me: "Always keep your bed nice, Frenzie darlin'…You'll never find a lost thing until you look where it is, not where you think it is…Waste not, want not." If I pulled the cat's tail, Margaret would admonish me: "Don't do that to the poor pussy cat, for you may be a pussy cat yourself some day." Or: "If the wind changes when you make that awful face, it will stick that way for the rest of your life."

Margaret had studied midwifery in Edinburgh. When I was a little older, I eavesdropped on her whispered conversations with the Irish maids about the forbidden subject of Having Babies. *Och!* The agony, and the blood, and the screams, and the boiling hot water in the kettle hung over the peat fire, and the swaddling of the crying bairn in clean towels, warmed on bricks that had been heated on the hearth. I was mystified and intrigued by the disjointed snatches I overheard, especially about some of the young mothers who were said to be "Bad." Why, I wondered? This was never explained.

I didn't know a thing about birth until I found the landmark issue of *Life* magazine (April 11, 1938) with its article "The Birth of a Baby," depicting the entire sequence in a series of detailed, but tantalizingly small photographs. To prevent me from reading it, my mother had torn the article out of our copy of *Life*, but I eventually saw it at a friend's house. Being a precocious reader, I had already skimmed through *Gone with the Wind*, but I had always thought that it was the baby breaking through her belly button that caused Melanie's agonizing experience in childbirth. Now the truth revealed seemed even worse, and incomprehensible. Where was that secret aperture, the baby's escape-hatch?

Another fascinating oddity about my "other mother" was that—in the perceived wisdom of the day, before she came over to America—Margaret had gone to a dentist to get all her teeth pulled out. Almost all our Irish maids had submitted to this as well. Scots, Brits and Irish had terrible teeth, because of diet, I suppose. All of the teeth were yanked out at the same time, uppers and lowers, and this resulted in horror stories told and retold. Men didn't want to marry women who still had their natural teeth, because of the inevitable expense to them after marriage. "Have you got your teeth?" the women would be asked, meaning their false teeth. The occasional sight of Margaret's teeth in a water glass at night, magnified by the water, was upsetting to me. I kept this knowledge secret from my mother and father, somehow fearing that they might make fun of her.

The Irish Catholics in our household were extremely superstitious, and their stories intrigued Marg even though she was a staunch Presbyterian. They got very worked up in the telling of their tales, the spooks and the "ghaists," and the wee folk that peopled their minds inevitably lurked in the corners of my imagination as well.

I have a vivid memory of being awakened on a hot summer night by a terrible thunderstorm. My mother and father were away, and all the Irish "girls" were awake. They congregated outside my room in the hall, keening and sobbing frightfully, as the crashing thunder and brilliant strobe lightning grew closer and closer. They recited their rosaries, calling on Holy Mary Mother of God to save us all from being burnt to cinders and ashes.

Even Margaret was scared, and came to hold me close, just as the huge sycamore tree in the circle at the front driveway was struck with an earsplitting crash, causing the windows to rattle. The keening of the Irish maids reached a scary doomsday crescendo, but the house did not catch on fire, everyone calmed down as the storm grumbled away, and perhaps their prayers did save us all.

On afternoons after school, when I was supposed to do my homework, Marg would bring a delicious hot dog and a big glass of milk to the nursery for me, only a few hours before my supper "to build me up." She was forever worrying that I was puny, unlike my cousin Minnie who would eat her dinner, and mine too, when she came to visit. (Minnie and I thought this a practical arrangement: it saved me from hiding bits behind the dining room curtains in the hopes the dogs would sniff them out before the waitress discovered the evidence.) I was not a big eater in those days.

I often refused to eat foods I disliked, especially prunes. One summer day I threw my prunes out of the dining room window when nobody was looking, and pretended I had eaten them. I was caught instantly, but it was a long time before I guessed how my crime was discovered: the prunes had pits, but my plate was bare.

I walked up to the Cadwaladers' big house on the hill to play almost every day, and Margaret enjoyed socializing with their help while I was having fun with my cousins. One memorable day she was gossiping away with my Aunt Mae's lady's maid, watching as she laid out the jewelry that my aunt was going to wear to a big party that night. "Will you look at the gorgeous diamond necklace, now? I wonder how it would be to wear such a thing to a dance?" says Marg. "Here, try it on," urged my aunt's maid, and she fastened the clasp around her neck, where it hung down incongruously over her white uniform.

"My, aren't I the foine lady," said Marg, and she tried a few jig steps about the bedroom. They both laughed, and then, panic! They couldn't undo it. The clasp was firmly stuck. Finally, desperate, they called downstairs to Barrett, the Cadwaladers' English butler, who, furious at their unseemly high jinks, tried unsuccessfully to work it loose, sweating and cursing.

"Hurry, hurry, the Madame will be home any minute! What if we're caught?" Just in the nick of time, as they heard the big town car coming up the drive, the stubborn fastening came apart, and my aunt never knew about the near thing. If she had, I'm certain that just like my own mother, she would have seen the funny side. Both sisters were always very loving and understanding with their staff.

Margaret made her escape from the bedroom down the back stairs as my aunt came up the front. The diamonds were replaced in their blue velvet case, and the little adventure was kept secret for a long time.

# 6

## *House Calls and the Dentist*

Once each week, I was subjected to a horrible thick chalky tablespoonful of milk of magnesia to "sweeten up" my stomach. This was on top of the daily pitched battle over a brimming fishy-smelling tablespoon of cod liver oil. No matter how far I backed into the corner and clenched my teeth, it somehow always went down "the red lane." I still remember fingers pinching my nose shut, and the spoon forcing its way between my lips and prying open my teeth.

There weren't many remedies in the medicine chests in those days. My father used to sniff up great snorts of warm salt water to relieve his hay fever, and when Mummy sometimes complained of feeling "liverish," she resorted to a disgusting sounding cure called a "blue mass pill," or at least that's what it sounded like to me. I hated to think about it. She sometimes threatened to go away for a "cure," which her lady friends seemed to believe in having periodically, but she never actually went along with them.

There was bicarbonate of soda for upset stomachs, aspirin for headaches, and vile dark brown argyrol for eye trouble, as well as those awful laxatives, milk of magnesia, and castor oil. Iodine and bright red Mercurochrome were liberally applied to cuts and scrapes. There were no birth control pills or pain pills or anti-depressants.

Medicine always tasted bad when I was a child, and we had no Mary Poppins to change its flavor into peppermint or chocolate. Still, it was sort of fun to be sick when I was a little girl. First of all, I got to stay home from school…and then the doctor came to visit _me_. In those days doctors made house calls, and children weren't forced to wait interminably in dreary doctor's offices, exchanging germs with every cough, staring at lethargic goldfish and tattered, out-of-date *Weekly Readers*.

When I was little, I actually looked forward to the exciting visit of our doctor, who drove the nine miles from his Chestnut Hill office to make a bedside call. I was the center of attention for this important visit. Margaret tidied my bed and changed into a freshly starched white uniform, and my mother cancelled her appointments to be on hand for the verdict.

Dr. Stiles drove up in his shiny Chevrolet coupe, never quite on time due to the distances between his many house calls. The tension would build for me, straining to hear the whispered discussion out in the hall, while my mother or Margaret gave him the lowdown on my symptoms, condition of my bowels, stomach upset, any fever or other complaints. Finally he came into my bedroom, carrying his black valise, with its important brass padlock, bringing with him an antiseptic smell, mingled with the refreshing cold air still clinging to his ankle length tweed overcoat.

Dr. Stiles was the young assistant to my paternal grandfather, the much loved and respected Dr. Radcliffe Cheston. Grandfather was an internist of the country doctor school who treated a wide spectrum of illnesses—strokes, heart trouble, appendicitis, every type of disease, and he delivered the babies as well.

Best of all, he was a wise and practical counselor to unhappy or troubled patients, long before the days of expensive shrinks and complicated analysts. Much later, my mother confided to me her acute embarrassment because her own father-in-law was her obstetrician, and brought me safely into the world. I don't think there was a distinction made between gynecologists and obstetricians at that time.

Every woman in our neighborhood wanted Dr. Cheston to deliver her babies. My mother had a great friend, Mrs. Chatfield, who was pregnant at the same time as she was. Dr. Cheston delivered me on July 22, his grandchild being his first priority, and then had to hop on the overnight Bar Harbor Express to rush up to Rockport, Maine to be at the lying-in of Mrs. C. He arrived in the nick of time to deliver her son Charlie. She always told my mother that she timed the birth, and waited until her favorite doctor could be there.

Actually I had few ailments that needed doctoring. In those days we didn't know about viruses, and everything respiratory was diagnosed as a cold, caused by a "germ." The most feared disease of those years was infantile paralysis...the dreaded *polio*. When there was an outbreak, usually in the summer, we children were kept at home and not allowed to go swimming. It was thought that swimming pools harbored that contagious illness.

Some of my schoolmates contracted whooping cough, mumps and chicken pox, and there were scattered cases of diphtheria, but I was lucky, and my only serious illness, when I was about nine, was measles, which then required a prison-like incarceration in a darkened room for two weeks. It came with a high fever, rash, and a grim warning that if I attempted to escape from my bed, blindness and deafness would inevitably result.

I could almost happily have spent the two weeks in bed reading, but this was forbidden to measles victims, for fear of eyestrain. To keep me occupied, Mummy and Margaret took turns reading to me, squinting at the text in the dim light. This was torture for me, a restless tomboy, who disliked being read to, because even at that early age I preferred to read to myself. Spending daytime in bed was boring, even with the gripping morning soap operas like *Mary Noble, Backstage Wife* on my little blue wooden radio, where it was always "tune in tomorrow" at the most dramatic moments.

My father had the splendid idea that pets would cure my boredom. The pets he chose for me were a surprise: *white rats!* They came to live in a cage, set up next to my bed. I examined them closely, trying to discover who was Jack and who was Jill.

I wasn't old enough yet to suspect that the "playing" of the rats was something more biologically complicated. Daddy put a loaf of homemade bread inside their cage, and they hollowed out a sort of Canyon de Chelly dwelling in it, chewing at their crumby walls, and twitching their pink whiskery noses.

For many years, Daddy was the president of the Philadelphia Zoo, and interested in all animals. He loved nature, and was a keen observer of wildlife and habitat, enthusiasms that he passed on to me, and that I have shared for the rest of my life.

In addition to our many dogs, we often kept exotic pets around the house that he had acquired from the zoo. At various times, our menagerie included baby alligators from the circus, a kinkajou that terrified the cook, peering into her window with his huge nocturnal eyes, a rhesus monkey that hated my brother and shrieked when he saw him, a parrot who tricked the dogs by whistling for them, and—for a short time—a beautiful young ocelot with gleaming black and yellow spotted fur, which lived in a box stall in the barn, that smelled strongly of cat. We couldn't tame her, and she hissed and bared her teeth when we approached.

We kept a succession of pet coons that rode around on my shoulder, and played with my ears and hair with their sensitive little hands, and a funny thieving crow, which roosted in a pine tree outside the back door. George once made a frog hotel out of an orange crate, and we had a splendid time collecting them from the stream, although the frogs didn't seem to enjoy their vacation very much. The biggest one skinned his nose in an abortive attempt at escape, and I rushed to paint the scrape with Mercurochrome, employing my best professional nurse technique. A buck rabbit left over from Easter grew to tremendous size and ferocity. He used to stand up on his hind legs, and strike out at me and growl when I tried to feed him his carrots.

Daddy often arranged behind-the-scenes tours for us at the Philadelphia Zoo. Once, my sister and I took turns cradling Bamboo, a tiny, furry, baby gorilla, in our arms. That baby grew to become the biggest gorilla then in captivity, before Gargantua took the title. I perched on a Galapagos turtle, let the baby elephant snuffle me with his trunk, and had great swaying rides on the big, kindly mother elephant. I remember measuring the depth of the cracks in the hide on her back with my bobby pin. So, tame rats in a cage by my bed seemed like a visit from my Zoo friends, and slightly more manageable for a bedroom.

Whenever I was alone, I would let the rats out of their cage to tunnel around in my tousled bedclothes, under and over the pyramid made by my raised knees. My brother once told me that if you held up a guinea pig by his tail, his eyes would drop out. Not realizing that guinea pigs had no tails, I tried the experiment with one of my rats to see what would happen, but luckily his eyes stayed attached, and he didn't seem to mind much, as I swung him to and fro by his long pink tail.

After a while, the cage began to give off a strong, musty, mouse-dropping smell, and one morning, to my distress, my companions were gone. I liked to think they had caught my measles, and they took my spots with them, and that somewhere in the world a kid was playing with a pair of red and white polka-dotted rats. Anyway, the next day up went the blinds, and my confinement was over. Afterwards, as a reward for my ordeal, I was given a fat piebald pony named (of course) Measles.

When I had my colds, Dr. Stiles would sit on the edge of my bed, pull up the top of my Best & Co. white flannel pajamas, and listen to my chest with his rubber-tube stethoscope. Its metal funnel felt cold on my skin, and tickled me, as I obediently took deep breaths; afterwards he always let me listen to my own particular internal rumblings. He then strapped the shiny round mirror with a hole in its center around his head and focused a point of light down my gullet. "Say AAAH"…Gag…AARGH. Diagnosis: "You've got yourself a nice red throat there, little lady." As if I didn't know.

Then he would start thumping, two fingers placed on my chest and back, rapping them sharply with the fingers of the other hand. This technique was copied later by some of us girls in our secret, mysteriously exciting games of "Doctor":

"Tell me where it hurts: Here? Here? How about DOWN HERE?" *Thump, Thump.* "Oh! Yes, doctor!" *Giggle, Giggle,* as the Place was touched. "Now it's my turn!"

All the odd things Dr. Stiles kept in his case fascinated me, and he took the time to show me the different instruments and gadgets. There were little glass bottles, strapped to the sides of the case with leather bands; rolls of cotton in blue paper wrappings, and stacks of those gagging wooden tongue depressors.

The doctor's treatment for stuffed-up noses was to grasp a thin wad of cotton between the jaws of a long shiny pincer-like tool, dip it into some sort of astringent solution from one of the many silver-capped bottles, insert the cotton strip way up nearly to the sinus cavity, and leave it there for at least twenty minutes, the dripping ends protruding from my nostrils like strange white mustachios.

Once the cotton snakes were pulled out, merciful breathing through my nose could begin. But after a few hours the rebound effect blocked the passages worse than ever.

If my chest was congested, the orders were for a burning hot mustard plaster before bedtime, or else Vicks VapoRub. This came in a blue glass jar, and Margaret scrubbed the yellow pungent ointment onto my chest with great force, as though she was polishing the furniture. Then I would be swaddled with a flannel towel pinned securely around my chest, left sweating and wheezing to breathe in the remedial fumes overnight.

Happily, I only remember one earache, and its horribly painful treatment of warm oil poured in my ear hole through a kitchen funnel. There was no penicillin in those days.

Another bad time came when the milk of magnesia didn't do its job, and Dr. Stiles prescribed an enema. Next came a wild scene, with Margaret and Peggy the chambermaid holding me down, the nasty red rubber tube spouting warm soapy water all over the bedclothes, the bedside lamp kicked over by my flailing feet; mission *not* accomplished! Nature eventually took its course, thanks to the odious administration of extra magnesia. In those days, adults expected children's bowels to run on time, like clockwork, and the embarrassing daily inspection of results was mandatory.

A terrible betrayal was foisted on me when I was taken to the Chestnut Hill Hospital for a tonsillectomy. This operation was deemed necessary for all children in those days. My mother and father assured me that I was going to the movies, a tremendous treat at age five, and that there would be ice cream afterwards.

I was told later that it took a doctor and two nurses to hold me down, trying to subdue me after I pushed the sickening ether-soaked cone off my nose before it could put me to sleep, and I went berserk. I was a very strong little girl. I got the ice cream all right, but my throat was too sore and bloody to swallow it, and the ether made me throw up.

The most dreaded medical experience of all was a trip to...*the dentist*. In those pre-fluoride years, I had terrible cavities, and I had to make many visits into Philadelphia to our dentist Dr. Fox, a gentle long-suffering man.

It took about an hour and a half to drive into town. Our route wound through lovely wooded Fairmount Park, along the shore of the Schuylkill River where the crews from the University of Pennsylvania and Temple University were often practicing in their long graceful shells, past the picturesque 19th century Rowing Club boathouses. We emerged in the big square in front of the imposing classical façade of the Philadelphia Museum of Art, dominated by the statue of William Penn standing on top of his high pedestal, the State Charter rolled under his arm, proudly surveying his City of Brotherly Love.

Dr. Fox often let me play with the mercury he used in the preparation of silver fillings, rolling the blobs of quicksilver all over the little round table where he kept his instruments, and then he would give me some to take home in a corked glass vial. I would dump it out onto my work table and let it roll all about, watching with fascination as it shattered into tiny balls, then amalgamated itself again, picking up dust and hairs. Back then, no one worried about the dangers of mercury poisoning.

Dr. Fox also let me pick up cotton rolls with his tweezers, and once I tried to stuff one in his ear in self-defense, while he was grinding away on a tooth with a large burr, like something you might use in woodworking class. The burr made my whole head vibrate, and it easily could have been used to jackhammer a pavement. Even worse was the fine curved pick, which probed the tender soft spots: "Open a little wider, Francie." OW! "Does that hurt?" OW! OW!

I don't know how Dr. Fox put up with me. Novocaine was seldom used back then for simple fillings. When it was, the needle seemed to be as big as the ones that veterinarians used to worm horses. I just had to be brave and not flinch too violently.

On the way home from the dentist, Margaret and I invariably stopped at a delicious smelling French bakery, where Marg bought me my favorite iced cakes—petit fours—and also *langues du chat*, delicate, flat cookies shaped like a cat's tongue.

It seems irrational now to think of going to the dentist to get painful cavities filled up, and then to go straight out and munch on sugary cookies, but actually these treats were delicious bribes that made the long car trip all the way into Philadelphia, and back again, something to look forward to. (Sort of.)

When I was a little older, I had to go to a *band dentist*...now called an orthodontist. Dr. Jackson tolerated no nonsense, and took no prisoners. He was a small, hunchbacked, balding man, with fuzzy sideburns who wore a starched, side-buttoned, short-sleeved tunic like a Mao jacket, which showed off his brawny, hairy forearms. He looked like one of Dr. Frankenstein's assistants, as he bent over me, his yellow fangs approaching my face: "Open wider, now, and we'll just tighten these up a bit." Taking a pair of pliers from his rack of sinister torture instruments, he twisted a little screw on the metal bands around each of my teeth until I yelped for mercy.

It took at least two days for the ache to let up after he got through with me. And it hurt too much to chew anything, even those soft "bribery" cookies. Until I outgrew orthodontics, my smile looked like the Brooklyn Bridge.

Once, while playing badminton, reaching open-mouthed for a high shot, I accidentally hooked one of the bands on my front teeth in the net. There I stayed, snared, while my opponent laughed and laughed and refused to help untangle me. It was a real crime to break the dental appliance, because it necessitated another trip to Philadelphia for expensive repairs, but the only way I could get myself unhooked was to twist it off.

When the bands were finally removed, my agony wasn't over yet. Dr. Frankenstein had a dreadful surprise: a retainer, to be worn every night so my teeth wouldn't relapse into their previous snaggles. He warned me that only the constant use of this retainer would save me from turning into Charlie McCarthy's buck-toothed sidekick, Mortimer Snerd.

The retainer was a nasty, slippery plastic gadget, which fitted into the roof of my mouth, with a single wire across the front teeth, and always smelled like early morning breath, no matter how often I rinsed it. I was always losing it, and feared that some guest might discover it behind the sofa cushions, hooked in the material—Yuck! If you misplaced it for too long, it wouldn't fit properly, and that made another trip to Dr. Frankenstein mandatory. After all that, my teeth are still fairly crooked.

My cousins Francis and Howard Gowen suffered through the same treatment, with the same orthodontic torture-master. To this day, sixty-odd years later, we still cringe at the memory of Dr. Jackson. Francis is a talented artist, and he used to amuse us by drawing comic strips featuring our fiendish dentist as the villain, bent over his cringing victim with huge red-hot pliers in his hand.

The stoicism I was forced to learn as I endured those painful appointments has stayed with me all these years. So far, fortunately, "pain medication" has rarely been included in my medicine cabinet. There will come a time when I will need to give in. And it will surely come.

# 7

## *Books and Tune in to Yesterday*

The best part of being sick in bed was when my mother came up to the third floor to visit me, bringing a parcel neatly wrapped in shiny mauve paper, from the Chestnut Hill Book Shop.

I read voraciously. Outside in my tree house, under the covers at night, on the seacoast rocks in Maine, or even in the car, knowing well it would make me horribly carsick, but unable to stop myself.

Perhaps it would be the latest *Oz* book, or a Nancy Drew mystery, or one of the Twins series. These were novels by Lucy Fitch-Perkins, about mischievous boy/girl twins who had all sorts of exciting adventures in their native lands. Each set of twins came from a different country—Dutch Twins, Mexican Twins, Italian Twins, Scotch Twins and even the prehistoric Cave Twins. The French Twins and the Belgian Twins lived in wartime Europe. Each book was packed with cultural, historical and geographical information, far easier to absorb than school geography lessons, because the stories were about real everyday lives of foreign kids my age.

I read and re-read *The Wind in the Willows*, *Doctor Dolittle*, *The Water Babies*, *Peter Pan*, Albert Payson Terhune's dog stories, and the enthralling tale *Swallows and Amazons* by Arthur Ransome, about the adventures of an intrepid family tribe of English children. The Newberry Award books came with a gold prize seal that you could peel from its cover and stick onto your pajamas like a medal.

Another favorite of mine, *The Princess and the Goblins*, was a thrilling story about an unlikely friendship between a young coal miner (Curdie), his fierce yellow dog Lena, a beautiful young princess, and their escape from sinister, hunchbacked goblins.

While fleeing, they get lost in a castle tower, and encounter a strange old lady with snow white hair and skin, who forces Curdie to hold his hands in the flames of her fireplace. Surprisingly, the flames are cool, and after the ordeal he is able to judge the character of a person by shaking hands. Instead of normal fingers, he might feel the rough paw of a beast, and know to beware. You never forget spooky details like that.

Over the years my father gave me books like a fat red volume of *The Complete Adventures of Sherlock Holmes,* and Kipling's *Just So Stories* and *The Jungle Books*, and *Captains Courageous*, *The Adventures of Tom Sawyer* and volume after volume of the *Oz* books. They absorbed me for hours and hours on end.

Books like these were my constant companions, and I lived in a world peopled by their characters. At night I put myself to sleep by inserting myself into the stories I read by daylight, performing great deeds of heroism, although the tangled tales often surfaced in wild nightmares. Dreadful things lived under my bed, and in the cupboard. If I were to stick a foot carelessly out over the edge of the bed, or let an arm hang down, bony hands would grab me and sharp teeth would rasp.

A constant shadowy presence crouched impatiently, waiting, waiting, in the big wing chair in the corner of my bedroom. I never managed to actually see him, or IT…but I would wake in terror and shout for faithful Marg to come from her bedroom next door to rescue me. My quavering calls for help resulted in many false alarms, with never a sign of the monster when the lights went on. Not so much as a claw-mark or footprint left behind to prove its stealthy visit.

My bedroom was big, with a row of three windows across the front, and another window on the side. During the night shadow patterns shifted across the walls, scrabbling branches rapped and scraped, and mysterious squeaks, creaks and cracks fed my imagination. In the daytime it was a fine bright room, and in summer it was reassuring to be woken by familiar sounds like the whirr of a hand-pushed lawn mower, the twitter of birdsong, and to smell the moist green of freshly cut grass. Then the night's terror was remote, and instantly forgotten.

Big Little Books were my favorites. These were books shaped like a cube, between hard cardboard covers, and just the right size to hold in a child's hands. Open a Big Little Book anywhere in its thick middle, and there you would find a page of large-print text opposite a vivid black-and-white drawing illustrating the action. Many of the stories were taken from the comics, or "funnies," as we then called them. I couldn't wait for the next volumes starring Dick Tracy, Tarzan, Terry and the Pirates, Little Orphan Annie, and Buck Rogers, as well as classic tales such as *Robinson Crusoe* and *Kidnapped.* I collected at least fifty, which I stored in a special Big Little Cupboard in my room.

The evocative illustrations in classic hardcover books—by artists like N.C. Wyeth, Ernest Shepherd and Arthur Rackham—are imbedded in my memory, and their images have been far more lasting than any subsequent ones from TV or cinema. Who could ever forget the pirates from *Treasure Island,* like blind Smee and Long John Silver, brandishing long, curved cutlasses, their wide canvas trousers flapping, bandanas on their pigtailed heads, with wicked knives clenched between their teeth?

The stories in Grimm's fairy tales, Edgar Allan Poe's *Tales of Mystery and Imagination,* Bram Stoker's *Dracula* and the cautionary tales of the German storybook *Struwwelpeter* ("Slovenly Peter") were gory and macabre. In *Struwwelpeter* a naughty boy won't stop sucking his thumb. His mother goes out, and…

> *The door flew open, in he ran,*
> *The great, long, red-legged scissor-man.*

> *Oh! Children, see! The tailor's come*
> *And caught our little Suck-a-Thumb.*
> *Snip! Snap! Snip! The scissors go;*
> *And Conrad cries out Oh! Oh! Oh!*
> *Snip! Snap! Snip! They go so fast;*
> *That both his thumbs are off at last.*

The illustration showed the sinister tailor leaping at little Conrad, seizing his thumbs between the blades of his enormous shears, the severed thumbs in a pool of blood on the floor. Unforgettable!

Another frightening scene that I recall from my storybooks was when Bluebeard's eighth wife found the key to the forbidden chamber, and unlocked the last door, only to behold the ghastly sight of a wall lined with iron meat hooks, on which hung the bloody heads of the other seven wives. Their long hair was trailing, their mouths were open in silent screams, and I fancied that the heavy smell of clotted blood hung in the stale air.

In the fairy tales, supposedly for little children, two-headed giants and ugly bristle-faced ogres routinely devoured brave little boys. Stepmothers were always wicked, and sent their stepchildren off on dangerous errands, hoping they would never find their way home again. A witch, who lived in an enticing Gingerbread House, captured a young brother and sister, Hansel and Gretel, intending to roast them alive in her oven after locking them up in a cage, and fattening them up for her feast. Another witch, a Russian one called BabaYaga, lived in a scary hut, mounted on chicken legs, in which she roamed around the forest searching for children to eat.

Poor Sleeping Beauty was given an injection by a jealous uninvited guest that put her into a coma for a hundred years. Snow White was given a poisoned apple to eat by her stepmother, the jealous queen, which also sent her into a drugged sleep. She was found by seven strange little dwarfs, who fell in love with her and kept her in a glass coffin in their kitchen, until the Prince finally came. Talk about weird tales! I thought them to be literally true, and never sought the deeper psychological meanings.

Television can never surpass those old stories for the sheer creative terror formed in a child's imagination. The scarier the better, and I loved hearing them, and reading them over and over again, never tiring of the repetition.

Of course there were the "girl" books too. I read the whole collection of Nancy Drew mysteries and the *Bobbsey Twins,* and Cinderella stories like *Sarah*

*Crewe (The Little Princess), Pollyanna, Black Beauty* and *The Secret Garden*. The themes were similar and intensely moralistic. The sweet, impossibly good young heroines were treated badly by cruel headmistresses or stepmothers, but they always triumphed on the tear-soaked last page.

Many other memorable stories of that time followed the same moralistic pattern. The young horsewoman Velvet wins the Grand National through sheer perseverance, Black Beauty is rescued from a cruel life of toil, and even that sissy Lord Fauntleroy gains the affection of his crusty old grandfather. Cinderella wins her Prince, and the spoiled hero of *Captains Courageous* learns what it takes to become a man. *Alice in Wonderland* was in a class by itself, and I don't remember appreciating it until I was much older.

My books taught me about the rewards of working hard, and being kind to everyone, but it was a long time before I came to understand that happy endings didn't always happen in real life, in spite of the best intentions.

Another escape from humdrum real life was my never-to-be-missed radio programs. I always finished my homework as fast as possible, for only then was I allowed to tune in. In those days, exciting serials were broadcast every weekday evening in fifteen-minute segments, each preceded by its own memorable jingle or theme song. The programs began about 5 p.m., and I listened with my ear close to my radio, while eating supper on a tray in my bedroom.

> *When it's Ralston time at breakfast,*
> *Then it surely is a treat*
> *To have some rich full-flavored Ralston*
> *Made from golden Western wheat.*
> *Won't you try it, you'll say buy it.*
> *Tom Mix says it's swell to eat.*
> *Jane and Jimmy too say it's best for you.*
> *Ralston Cereal can't be beat.*

That jingle introduced the adventures of Tom Mix, the noble cowboy, and Jane and Jimmy, the two lucky children who lived on his ranch. After Tom came *Little Orphan Annie*. I had talked the cook into ordering several tins of Ovaltine, which no one in our house ever drank, in order to get the metal seal necessary to send away for all the exciting premiums the announcer pitched during each installment. It took at least three seals to earn the Little Orphan Annie Shake Up

Mug, which he insisted was the perfect thing for drinking Ovaltine. Just one problem: although I coveted the mug, I hated Ovaltine.

Many tins later I had enough seals to send away for the Secret Decoding Pin, which I needed in order to decode the important massage given at the end of each night's episode. This was a flashy gold medallion with a revolving wheel containing letters and numbers, which when properly lined up, revealed the clue for next time's action. The jingle went:

> *Who's the little chatterbox, the one with curly auburn locks?*
> *Who could she be? It's Little Orphan Annie.*
> *Always wears a sunny smile, now wouldn't it be worth your while*
> *If you could be…like Little Orphan Annie?*
> *"Arf!" says Sandy* [who always agreed with his bossy little mistress].

Ageless Annie was indeed brave and resourceful. With the benign protection of her millionaire guardian Daddy Warbucks, his seven-foot tall turbaned servant Punjab, and the wily oriental Asp, backed up by loyal Sandy, Annie challenged her evil opponents to do their worst. The adventures were thrilling, and each episode ended with a cliffhanger, and Annie's trademark exclamation, "Leapin' Lizards!"

I joined the Buck Rogers Space Squadron, but in order to advance in rank I had to persuade the cook that our household actually needed more chocolate flavored drink powder, Cocomalt, this time. I think I made it as far up the ladder as lieutenant before the cook put her foot down and said there was not an inch of room on the shelf for any more opened and untasted tins of anything, so I never could get my official Buck Rogers Jet Propelled Flying Belt. This was probably fortunate, as it may not have worked quite as well for launching myself off the roof of the pump house as I had imagined.

The sound effects that accompanied the radio programs were wonderfully realistic: crackling fires, pouring rain, galloping hooves, creaking doors, howling dogs and squalling cats, gunshots, and the muffled "OOF" sounds of punches hitting solar plexuses.

You could send away for your very own sound-effects kit, and it was most satisfactory to wave a sheet of tin to create thunder, or pour sand on it and make rain. Crumpling cellophane made fire, and rubber suction cups on the ends of sticks sounded like galloping hooves when properly synchronized. In fact, sending away for stuff was wonderful fun, and a major preoccupation. First you chose the item you couldn't do without, listed in the Johnson & Smith catalogue from Racine, Wisconsin. The ads were irresistible. *"You too can learn to be a Ventrilo-*

*quist, astound your friends, and throw your voice."* The drawing showed a young boy staring at a padlocked steamer trunk from which issued a pitiful voice crying, "Let Me Out, Let Me Out."

Another item was the wonderful Look Back Ro Scope. This was a periscope gadget that allowed you to look over your shoulder to spot an assassin who might be following you. The catalogue also offered itching powder, dribble glasses, whoopee cushions, snapping gum packages, exploding cigarettes, and disappearing ink; all hilarious tricks to be played on the long-suffering staff and jaded older brothers and sisters.

I had to save up my meager allowance (25 cents per week) to collect the amount needed "in coin or stamp," and then, once that was mailed off, weeks of incredible suspense crawled by waiting for the package, checking the post every day.

When the brown cardboard box finally arrived, there was almost always keen frustration. That ventriloquist kit consisted of a little serrated leather and metal thing that you were supposed to hold in your mouth until the leather softened, pressing it against the roof of your mouth with your tongue and "talking" with your lips pressed tight shut. The only result was a sort of squawky bird whistle. But these disappointments never lasted for long; there was always another desperately wanted item to send away for.

Another program never to be missed even if there was a test at school the next day was *The Adventures of Dick Tracy*. His lengthy romance with fiancée Tess Trueheart was never consummated because Dick was always far too busy eliminating crime. His memorable opponents like the Brow, and Prune Face, and his eccentric collaborators Gravel Gertie, B.O. Plenty, Vitamin Smith, and his loyal young sidekick Junior, kept every episode lively. (The same characters were illustrated in the Sunday comics so you could picture how every one really looked.)

His marvelous two-way radio is now available to everyone as a cell phone or a BlackBerry, but Chester Gould, Dick Tracy's original cartoonist, had already invented its counterpart in the 1930's. His model was even better, because it could be worn on the wrist and thus concealed under the coat sleeve when necessary to mutter emergency information.

Then came Jack Armstrong, the All-American Boy, whose jingle went:

> *Wave the flag for Hudson High Boys, show them how we stand,*
> *Ever shall our team be champions, known throughout the land!*
> *Won't you try Wheaties? Just buy Wheaties,*
> *The best breakfast food in the land!*
> *Jack Armstrong! Jack Armstrong! Jack Armstrong! RAH! RAH! RAH!*

Jack was impossibly good, true, and noble, so my radio loyalty demanded that he too be given shelf space. I absolutely had to have those precious box tops from the Wheaties packages. People may think that television invented marketing aimed at children, but we kids were already vulnerable and all too susceptible victims in those days.

On Sunday nights, the Lone Ranger arrived to the resounding accompaniment of galloping hooves and the *William Tell Overture*. Loyal Tonto was always waiting on the trail ahead for the Masked Man's shout of "Git 'em up Scout" and a hearty, "Hi ho Silver, Awaaaay."

Then the long drawn-out scary sound of a squeaky door ushered me into the "Inner Sanctum," where the morgue-voiced host narrated terrifying mystery stories of murder and mayhem. My last permitted program, *The Shadow* followed. *"The weed of crime bears bitter fruit. Who knows what evil lurks in the hearts of men? The Shadow knows!"* After that captivating introduction, the Shadow, his devoted assistant Margo Lane and faithful manservant Cato were off on another daring Crusade Against Crime.

The times my mother and father were actually at home, they always climbed up to the third floor to kiss me good night after my programs. Mummy's long silky tea-gown sleeves, perfumed deliciously with Chanel #5, tickled my nose as she bent down to kiss me, and Daddy teased by rubbing his scratchy face against my cheek. I wriggled and giggled and made many attempts to prolong the "good nights" by dreaming up unnecessary and imaginative questions.

Finally, I was urged to say my prayers, hands folded, eyes shut tight, starting with "Our Father who art in Heaven," followed by "Now I lay me down to sleep." I hated this gloomy prayer because it ended with "If I should die before I wake, I pray the Lord my soul to take." Not a very comforting idea for a little girl to think about during the long night ahead.

My bedtime add-on prayers were then made as lengthy as possible, listing at least ten family members, Margaret, best friends, dogs and pets, and as many personal desires as I could work in…("Please God make it so that I can go to…whatever movie was playing next week.") My father frowned on these shopping lists to God, and warned me that God was much too busy with His important concerns to be bothered with such trivial requests as a kid wanting to go to the movies.

Until I was about ten years old, the bedroom lights were turned out at eight o'clock on school nights, with the exception of Sundays on account of *The Shadow*. Children, in general, didn't stay up late in those days, although there was always forbidden reading by flashlight under the covers, mine judiciously thwarted by Marg, after fifteen minutes or so. "Och, you'll ruin your eyes doin' that." Flashlight confiscated.

Margaret was often responsible for my pets. I was negligent about taking care of them, in spite of repeated warnings that they would be sold or given away to more responsible and well-behaved children like the despised Jacqueline of the golden curls, who always lurked in the background ready to humiliate and infuriate me.

Polly the parrot's messy cage had to be cleaned, and Captain our singing canary had to have water and seed. If he escaped, as he often did, he had to be caught and returned to his perch before my Scottie got him. The smelly turtle and goldfish water had to be changed and their bowls scrubbed, and the baby alligators had to be retrieved from behind the radiators where they sometimes crawled to welcome warmth.

The one pet Marg couldn't tolerate was Mike, my rhesus monkey. He was most engaging, with his bright eyes and black-masked face, but he was too fast for her, or anyone for that matter. One hot summer afternoon when I was walking around the garden with Mike on my shoulder, his habitual perch, I was called over to the porch where my mother and father and the Cadwaladers and other guests were sitting in front of a tray of iced tea and mint juleps.

Uncle Gouvie, a rotund and fastidious gourmet, dressed as impeccably as always for the warm weather in striped shirt, white linen suit and silk bowtie, was preparing to cut into a luscious, runny, pungent, and perfectly aged Camembert he had brought especially for the occasion.

With the lightning speed of all monkeys, Mike leapt off my shoulder onto the table, and shoved both his hands into the creamy cheese. The pearly goo squelched up between his fingers, and he brought them dripping to his nose. Smelling his hands, and baring his yellow teeth in a comical expression of disgust, Mike flicked his wrists, and the cheese spattered all over my uncle's tie and shirt. He and my father were furious, but my mother and Aunt Mae, although making noises of sympathy, couldn't hide their laughter. My uncle's discomfiture only made the scene more hilarious to them; off they went into their usual gales of laughter, which made matters even worse.

Feeling responsible, I was embarrassed and scared, because now Mike was jumping around and shrieking, up and over the chairs, the drinks were spilling, and I couldn't catch him. I thought for sure he would be taken away from me and banished forever for his bad monkey behavior. But after he had broken up the party, he was allowed to stay with me until we left for Maine, when they took him back to the Philadelphia Zoo to rejoin his rhesus cousins.

# 8

## *Toys, Games and School Days*

I had wonderful toys when I was small, but when I was too young to run an electric train set of my own, I had fun watching my brother George fooling around with his narrow gauge Lionel set. The tracks twisted and looped around his bedroom, under the beds and chairs. The rocky papier-mâché tunnels and painted snow-capped mountains, metal trestle bridges and the neat tin stations with their window boxes of red geraniums created a whole make-believe world. He often rigged dramatic train wrecks, sending the huffing steam engine hurtling into the passenger cars, whose lighted windows revealed unsuspecting travelers peacefully reading their newspapers. Then, suddenly…CRASH! Tiny sparks flew, a sharp smell of burning ozone came from the transformer, and the cars had to be lifted back on the track, and painstakingly hooked together again. Fortunately the passengers remained unscathed, stoically waiting for their next adventure.

Once George got a long extension cord and connected a track on the lawn outside the library. He arranged the stations, placed firecrackers with long fuses inside the little shelters, and blew them up into scorched fragments just as the train approached. The dogs barked, and hid in the bushes, except for the time that Maggie, our intrepid fox terrier, snatched up a sizzling cracker and ran off with it, luckily dropping it before it blew up. The successful demolition of the station buildings was exciting, but when our father found out later, he was furious. George was lambasted for wanton destruction of property, and a waste of money, to say nothing of the danger to the dogs and kid sister.

I always loved trains, and I knew about them intimately, because of our frequent travels to South Carolina and Maine. One of my very favorite toys was a two-foot-long model of a sleeping car on wheels. It was an exact replica of a Pullman right down to the plush upholstery, the upper berth that pulled down, the green and red striped mattress and beige blankets, and the hidden toilet under one of the seats. Stuffed animals and dolls loved taking rides around the nursery in their private sleeping car.

I also remember a foot-long metal swimming pool that I could fill with water. It had adjacent dressing rooms, a diving board and swim ladder, and some little wooden swimmers who floated about happily, or lay on the tile-patterned edge in their one-piece bathing suits.

Another great toy was a tugboat that cruised and huffed in my bathtub. It had a real working steam engine, which ran by means of a candle placed under its tiny boiler. I was playing with this on December 11, 1936, while Marg was listening to my radio. It was the day of the worldwide broadcast of King Edward the Eighth's abdication speech. The handsome young monarch was beloved by Marg, and she listened to his speech with tears pouring down her cheeks. She had nothing good to say about Wallis, "that woman!"

I was too interested in the performance of my boat to pay attention that day, but I seldom tired of hearing Marg talk about the two little princesses, "Lillibet"—the future Queen, who was exactly my age—and her younger sister Margaret Rose. It seemed to me that Marg knew everything about what they wore and how they lived. She was insatiably curious about the Royals, and followed their lives with minute care. For her, the two princesses were "wee dolls," always dressed alike in snappy formal coat, hat and glove outfits, suitable for church…not like me in my tomboy blue jeans. Moreover, they had curly hair, like the despised Jacqueline.

I often played with a wood-burning kit. The soft wooden practice boards that came with the kit smelled powerfully of burning when I dug in the hot point. The smoke curled up, and my big work table became heavily scarred with initials and designs after the board itself was used up.

I doubt there were any warnings connected to this tool. Common sense prevailed, and I could burn my initials on anything wood or leather, within reason. How different from today when hair dryers have a tag attached permanently to the cord warning you not to drop them in the bathtub, and mattresses mysteriously threaten you with imprisonment if you remove their label: "DO NOT REMOVE THIS TAG."

The only successful experiment I remember performing with my chemistry set was the rotten-egg smelling sulfur bomb. The glass test tubes became heavily and permanently encrusted with all the ingredients mixed haphazardly together, and although the foaming beakers furnished hope for eventual alchemy or explosions, no youthful Madame Curie flourished up there in my third floor lab.

Once I mixed up a little bottle of eye drops (flour, water and peroxide) and squirted it into a doll's blue glass eyes with an eye dropper. When the concoction dried, it stuck her long eyelashes together in great globs, and stained her pink china cheeks with streaky white tears. I was not a successful RN, but I never liked that doll much anyway, with her goody-goody looks and lace dress. I was scolded because she turned out to be an expensive heirloom doll from Paris.

I occasionally played with the other dolls, especially one who was dressed as a Persian princess. I remember her now as an exotic forerunner of Barbie. She had a lovely china face, long straight black hair and a golden chain around her neck. She wore a green brocaded robe embroidered with seed pearls. Most interesting of all, underneath her first layer of petticoats, she wore a silken slip that had a padded bosom sewn into it! All my other girl dolls were completely devoid of any sexuality. There were no boy dolls in my bedroom except for Andy, Raggedy Ann's brother...and his overalls never came off.

There were always new toys for me at Christmas, but I was not permitted to open anything on Christmas morning until the family was awake. Of course I was up at six, sneaked downstairs before seven, and kept vigil outside the door to my parents' bedroom in the wintry darkness, waiting in trembling anticipation while my boring older brothers and sisters were, unimaginably, still asleep.

When the summons to enter was finally issued through the closed door, I bounded in to see the long-anticipated stockings hanging from my mother's bedroom mantelpiece and Daddy sitting on the edge of her bed. At last Christmas had really arrived. Two or three excited dogs sniffed at the lumps and bulges, because there were always good meaty bones stuffed inside for them, and each one had his own stocking, labeled in characteristic Santa handwriting. Those empty, but hopeful socks we had hung up on the Night Before Christmas had more than fulfilled their promise.

On one of those Christmas mornings when I was about five and still gullible, I actually "met" Santa. Daddy beckoned me into his room. "I have a wonderful surprise, Francie!" he said. The closet door sprang open, and with a loud "HO HO!" a jolly man popped out. He had fluffy white whiskers and was wearing a long red robe like St. Nicholas. He gave me a bear hug, asked me if I had been a good girl, hummed a tune, swept me up in a few waltz steps and vanished down the stairs. Afterwards the back hall staff told me that Santa gobbled down six fried eggs in our kitchen, whistled up his reindeer, and flew off over the rooftops! Being a True Believer, I was thrilled!

Much later, my parents told me that "Santa" had actually been my charming playboy Uncle John Fell, who had been up all night at a Christmas Eve party, quite tipsy, and dressed in my father's red flannel wrapper and some cotton wool whiskers that he had stuck on with shaving soap. Well, that explained why Santa Claus was wearing black patent leather dancing pumps.

A few years later, Christmas marked a sad loss of innocence for me when someone forgot to remove a price sticker from a toy, which I recognized from Miss Houston's five-and-ten. The awful truth dawned on me, but I kept up the pretense of Believing for years, for my family's sake, and also for mine, because I didn't want to give up the stocking gifts.

Years later, on Christmas mornings when my own four children lined up before entering the library, where the "stockings were hung by the chimney with care," I always felt a tingle of the same old magic, when the limp red stockings of Christmas Eve were revealed bulging with mysterious presents. Even though we had sat up half the night before, stuffing them, I could almost Believe again, through the eyes of our happy children.

An object of spooky fascination for me, whenever I could get my brother to take it out of its hiding place underneath the sweaters in his bureau drawer, was a shrunken head from Ecuador. He had bought it from a hotel waiter in Quito. The head was the size of a baseball, and the dark tan skin on its cheeks was covered with fine downy hair. The wide nostrils were plugged with cotton, the lips sewn together with twine, the eyelids were shut, and the hair on its head was long, coarse, and black. It was not exactly a toy for a ten-year-old girl.

Later on, my brother told me that he gave it to our nephews. Their mother, who was extremely religious, took the head to the Church of the Redeemer, and gave it a Good Christian Burial.

My friends and I played cutthroat games of Monopoly, and the Uncle Wiggly board game. None of us was above cheating a bit as we tried to escape the clutches of the Skillery Skallery Alligator and his grim penalty: GO BACK TO START! We also played Parcheesi, Snakes and Ladders, Slap Jack, Pounce, Jacks, and performed card tricks of all kinds…until the golden moment each evening when games were abandoned and radio programs came on.

Everyone had a cap pistol for gun battles—Good Guys vs. Bad Guys, Cowboys vs. Indians—and the smoky gunpowder smell from the red reels of caps as they exploded was titillating and delicious. We practiced many complicated falls when mortally wounded, some of our imaginative, agonizing death throes taking minutes, as our cruel murderers stood over us, gun smoking. "Now you DIE!"

We girls played marathon games of jacks, and my friend Barbara always won the complicated game called "fancies." She scooped up the jacks for "Cherries in the Basket" or "Jack be Nimble" with her delicate hands and long fingernails, easily beating the rest of us clumsy tomboys with our grubby short nails.

Minnie and I were fascinated by the Ouija board, and spent hours watching the little triangular platform scooting around over the letters and numbers printed on the smooth wooden surface of the board…Whenever it paused we would swear that we weren't manipulating it. One awful day, we asked Ouija whether Minnie's father, who had been ill for weeks, was going to die. The viewing glass raced to YES. We put away the board, scared and upset, and a short time later, Minnie was called home from school; her father was dead.

At school recess we skipped rope to complicated rhyming rhythms: "Teddy Bear, Teddy Bear, climb the stairs. Teddy Bear, Teddy Bear, say your Prayers." We also played Hopscotch, Tag, Simon Says, Statues, Still Pond No More Moving, or The Farmer takes a Wife, with its grim and embarrassing line for the last child left unchosen: *"The cheese stands alone, The cheese stands alone, Hi-Ho the Derry-O, the cheese stands alone!"* Somehow the abandoned cheese always managed to survive without too much trauma.

Valentine's Day at school was hard on the unpopular girls. There was a cardboard "mailbox" decorated with lacy doilies and red hearts, where you put your unsigned valentines, the envelopes addressed in disguised writing. The designated "mailman" called out the names of the lucky recipients, and in our small all-girl class it was painfully obvious who received the fewest.

We didn't have team sports like field hockey until I was about twelve. On stormy days when we couldn't go out to play, our lovely talented French teacher Mademoiselle Lambert taught us crewel embroidery, and such useful things as darning and buttonholes.

In study hall we were only permitted to read schoolbooks. Once I was caught, hiding a Nancy Drew mystery under my arithmetic book. When asked if I had done all my homework, I lied. Mrs. Comfort, our savvy English teacher, challenged me: "Well, then, Frances, just give me your workbooks. You won't be needing them at home, will you?" My blood froze. Caught in the act!

Next day, after a guilty sleepless night, I was summoned to the principal's office, where I tearfully confessed. I was assigned a double dose of homework for the next night. It taught me a lifelong lesson about confession being a better tactic than a tangled web of lies, which usually doubles the trouble. My mother admonished, "You'll never regret doing the right thing, Frances. And what's more, you'll always know for sure what it is, even if you're tempted to ignore your conscience."

There was no such thing as parent-teacher conferences, unless for emergencies. Teachers were a breed apart socially, and my mother had no contact with them, except I think, when she might have attended my graduation from eighth grade.

Birthday parties were great occasions, always held at a classmate's home, never at a commercial establishment. They featured complicated spider webs where you unraveled yards of criss-crossing strings to claim the prize at the end, or fishponds where you held a fish pole over a sheet tied between two trees, and wiggled it around until the "fish" (a neatly ribboned package) was hooked on by the grownup crouching behind the sheet. Pin the Tail on the Donkey was a fixture, as were three-legged races, sack races, and potato-in-the-spoon races.

Some birthday parties were more elaborate than others with magicians and clowns, and there was a memorable one at my friend Evie's house, which featured a trained cockatoo act, a supper of creamed chicken, peas and rice, and for dessert, spun sugar nests containing tiny vanilla, chocolate, and strawberry ice cream eggs. A nurse or a mother stayed in close attendance behind each chair, to keep order and mop up the spills.

Boys were strictly segregated from girls in separate schools. Except for my male cousins, the only time I officially consorted with these strange beings was at dancing class, starting when I was about twelve. I was self-conscious, and hated wearing the party dresses that were picked out for me by my mother from a selection brought to the house by an obnoxious husband-and-wife sales team named the Baders.

Mr. and Mrs. Bader would arrive at our house with a huge steamer trunk full of dresses. I had to strip down to my cotton underpants and undershirt, embarrassed and chilled, and try on dress after dress in our living room. My mother bought all my school dresses (and only one party dress) several sizes too large, with enormous hems, so that I had "room to grow into them." I was stuck with them for years. My own tastes were given no consideration.

I remember enduring the agony of sitting on the girls' bench at the Friday Afternoon Dancing Class, waiting disconsolately as the boys dashed across the polished floor of the Chestnut Hill Cricket Club ballroom, choosing just about every girl ahead of me. This ritual was a double shame for me. In my shyness I didn't want to be chosen, and yet it was a public humiliation at age eleven or twelve to be the girl who was picked last. The boys skidded to a halt in front of the row of seated girls, and they were then supposed to bow to their chosen one. If you were left out, a reluctant partner was shoved toward you by the dance mistress.

The ever-present Margaret sat with the other nurses and mothers at the far end of the room, motioning me frantically to "Keep yer knees together, Frenzie!" I used to sit there miserably, in my short frilly dress and white socks, with my feet firmly planted apart in their black patent leather slippers, as though I was still wearing blue jeans.

This humiliation was deepened by the fact that cousin Minnie, exactly my age, was always picked early. She knew more about boys than I did, having a brother only a few years older, who brought his friends home to play. After one of these awful evenings, I asked my mother what you talked to boys about. She said: "Get them to talk about themselves," which turned out to be a long-lasting piece of wisdom, very useful except during the actual "dancing."

Dancing? No, it was torture. The boys pumped their arms up and down as though desperately signaling a taxi to stop. They held their female partners with a grim and sweaty grasp, and the dance steps of the boys were usually set to a different rhythm from the tunes being played by the bored pianist in the corner. Conversation was out of the question until the lemonade and cookies arrived. It would have been like trying to talk while drowning.

Once at our school, in a desperate attempt to shape eight-year-old lumps into graceful ballerinas, the headmistress, Miss Zara, promoted modern dance. We had to wear awful Greek tunics, and twirl floaty Isadora Duncan scarves. The dance teacher was a strict, irascible Russian woman called Madame Kripska, who pounded out mangled Tchaikovsky on the battered school piano, calling out the rhythm in her harsh foreign accent—"123, 123"—as we bounded gracelessly around the auditorium; there was no gym at our school in those days.

Unable to stand it, Madame would leap up from the piano and grab us around our wrists, or pinch us unmercifully with her steely talons, goading us in a torrent of Russian and French to greater terpsichorean efforts. Our final recital, held outside on the lawn in the spring, must have broken her heart, for she did not return the next year.

School was fun. I did well in my lessons, and had lots of friends. Because my family's house was isolated from other properties, it was a treat for me to visit classmates who lived in neighborhoods, where I could walk to shops like Streeper's Drug Store for ice cream or Miss Houston's Department Store for comics, Big Little Books and hair bands. We loved to walk a few blocks to Warner's Shoe Shop, where we bought all our school shoes (always lace-up oxfords). Sneakers were only worn for tennis, because they supposedly didn't give enough support for growing feet. Mr. Warner, a jolly man, gray-haired and bespectacled, would let us look at our feet in his X-ray machine, even if we weren't there to buy anything.

In those days, shoe stores—especially the ones that sold children's shoes—often had fluoroscopes, or X-ray machines, so parents could see exactly how well their children's feet fitted into the shoes before making a purchase. You mounted a platform, and stuck your foot into a slot in the pedestal. Leaning your forehead on a padded headrest, you could see your own skeleton toes wiggling inside your shoes. X-rays were not known to be harmful back then, not deadly radiation as they are nowadays.

Roller skating on the sidewalks in Chestnut Hill was great fun. The skates had four heavy metal wheels fastened to an adjustable plate, which gripped the edges of our oxfords. A skate key, like a miniature socket wrench, was used for tightening them. It was a most valuable object, worn constantly on a string around the neck like a sacred talisman.

The only hard surface to be found around home was in the Cadwaladers' cement laundry yard, where I could grind along on my roller skates around and around under the clotheslines, dodging wet flapping sheets, and tripping over the cracks. There was nowhere to ride my bike except on the lawn, which was too difficult because in those days bikes had no gears. The gravel driveway at our house was too skiddy for bicycles, resulting in falls and skinned knees, with "Africa-shaped scabs," as I once heard them accurately described. All my Chestnut Hill schoolmates had plenty of practice whizzing around on the sidewalks, and I was ashamed of my wobbly performance when I joined them.

Until I was about twelve, we almost never went to stores to shop, except to Mr. Warner's for shoes. The awful Baders made their house calls twice a year to show dresses and formal "church coats." Pajamas, underwear, shorts and polo shirts were ordered from Best & Co.'s catalog. These never varied, year after year. Shorts were always navy blue with a white stripe down each side and two rows of buttons down the front.

Polo shirts came in light blue, white, yellow or striped, period, and I was not allowed to choose my preferences. Sweaters were knitted for me by Margaret. Everything for school was laid out on the bed each morning, and that was that; there was no argument. I did love my blue jeans. They were my regular weekend "uniform," and still are.

The barber, Mr. Redhouse, cut my hair at home until I was about twelve. He was a thin old man with one blue eye, and one brown. Mummy told me that one of his eyes was glass, but she didn't know which one...and I never found out, no matter how I stared. He arrived in an ancient flivver and set up his barbershop in her bedroom. He'd hoist me high up onto a teetering pile of cushions stacked on top of a chair, and wrap a long printed sheet around my neck while making odd chirping noises as he delivered a running monologue to keep me still and to divert my mind from his long sharp gleaming scissor blades. They reminded me of that luckless boy, Suck-a-Thumb. When he trimmed my bangs, the cold steel blades pressed against my forehead...Snip, snap, snip!

After flapping out the sheet, Mr. Redhouse powdered the back of my neck with a big tickly shaving brush to get rid of the itchy hairs, and then swept up the little piles of trimmings. He told me that he saved all the hair he cut, and put it outside his house so the birds could pick it up to line their nests. Whenever I found a bird's nest, I always examined it for a hairy lining, to no avail.

My mother and Aunt Mae bought all their linens and towels from an exceedingly boring woman called Miss McKenna, who visited us twice each year—in the summer in Maine, and in the winter at Sandy Run—arriving with huge steamer trunks of samples, carried in by a fat sweaty man who was either her slave or her husband or both.

Mummy and Aunt Mae would groan because their linen closets were already overflowing with monogrammed towels, washcloths and sheets, but they felt obligated to keep on purchasing linens from old Miss McKenna, because she had sold linens to my grandmother when my mother was a girl. I remember Mummy actually hiding so as not to face her, but she turned up persistently, usually the very next day.

The trouble with Miss McKenna was not the frequency of her visits, or her relentless salesmanship, but the indestructible quality of her linens. Fifty years later, I am still using a few of Mummy's monogrammed bath towels. They are rough, and see-through-thin, inefficiently small, but sentimentally "too good to throw away."

In spite of my parents' wealth, our habits were frugal by today's standards. Very few things were ever thrown away. Men's collars were turned, sheets and socks were darned, hems let down and raised, and lights snapped off as soon as one left the room. I had an unrealistically small allowance, and absolutely no knowledge about money. All practical needs were provided, but most requests for extras were refused.

My childhood was sheltered and over-protected. Outside our house, I overheard derogatory names like "mackerel snatchers," "yids," "kikes," "wops," and "niggers," but I never related these words to real people like our longtime Italian gardener, Dominick, or the Jewish girls at school, or my beloved "colored" friends on our South Carolina plantation. As far as I was concerned, the epithets were a kind of nickname that was never used in front of people of those ethnic backgrounds.

I was isolated from the real world outside of our charmed circle, but one memorable time when I was about ten, an exotic, exuberant relative of my mother's,

Cousin Tony Biddle came to call. He was well known for his eccentricities like keeping alligators in his living room, and he was a passionate amateur boxer and a Marine Corps Colonel. His daughter Cordelia Biddle Duke wrote an affectionate memoir about him, *The Happiest Millionare,* later made into a movie. That day, he told me vehemently that it wasn't too early to learn to protect myself from muggers, and proceeded to give me a lesson in self-defense on the spot.

He coached me professionally, posturing with cocked fists like Gentleman Jim Corbett. "Trick your opponent by leading with your right, and then giving him a left uppercut to the jaw." I practiced seriously, leaping up in the attempt to reach his jaw with the wild right and futile uppercut. I don't remember doing much damage due to the difference in our heights. Then came sinister lesson number two. "If he should succeed in tying you up, always keep your wrists perpendicular to each other so that the rope has some slack, and after the assassin or mugger leaves, you can wriggle your wrists free." He tied me up with clothesline and it worked, sort of. I don't believe he tied my arms behind my back with quite the tightness my mugger might have used. I have kept his advice firmly in my mind, but I've never had to put it into practice.

I was always oversensitive to any conflict. When I overheard a quarrel between my mother and father, I used to to run upstairs and hide because it upset me so. It was rare that they argued in front of me, and the disputes that I did listen to were usually about something trivial, like my mother hating to sign the checks for the household bills that he waved under her nose, usually just before dinner after he returned from the office. "No Cliffe, not now. I'll do them tomorrow." The times they did get angry, I always took my mother's side. Daddy's temper, and his sometimes peremptory orders to the help, saddened and scared me. To this day, I dislike giving orders to anyone. I remember writing an angry, tearful letter addressed to my father, accusing him of being mean, and threatening to run away forever if he wasn't nicer to my mother and the servants. I hadn't the courage to give it to him and hid it in a "secret" compartment in my desk. Later, when I looked for it, it was gone. Daddy probably found it, just as he discovered all my secrets.

My father had a short fuse, but I never doubted that he loved my mother dearly in spite of his attempts to make her more disciplined and more like his family, the Chestons, who were serious, practical and accomplished self-made successes, and not like the present generation Fells and Drexels, who were amusing, easygoing, and of a deferential, Quakerly politeness.

My Grandfather, DR Radcliffe Cheston,
and my father, Radcliffe Cheston Jr
at the wheel of Dr Cheston's 1910 Cadillac

DR Cheston's house, built in 1890
still stands at 102 West Chestnut Hill ave.

His mother, Grandmother Cheston, was upright, religious, and strict. She had white hair swept back in a bun, white skin, a long face, and always wore black after my grandfather died. At that time, their were strict rules for observing a death in the family; mourning bands were worn by men around their upper left sleeves, widows wore black, and notepaper was bordered in black for a year after a funeral. I was scared of Grandmother Cheston, and I sensed somehow that my mother didn't like her much either. Maybe Grandmother thought her daughter-in-law frivolous because of her comical sense of humor and popularity with men.

My grandfather, Dr. Cheston died when I was only about four, and my last memory of him was especially fond. He was recovering from a heart attack, and he invited me up onto his big mahogany bed to help unwrap a huge basket of fruit and jams that one of his devoted patients had sent him. Each orange or apple was wrapped up in green tissue paper and just like Christmas, the unwrapping was part of the fun. Digging down to the very bottom of the shredded packing, I finally came upon a little glass boot filled with candies. He hugged me and said, with a big wink, "You can have this, but don't open it." He was a great tease, because we both knew I would open the boot and devour its contents as soon as I had the chance. I kept the little boot—empty, of course—for many years.

Two of Grandfather's favorite admonitions were: "Pleasant dreams and sweet repose, cover your head but not your nose." I never could see how that was possible, although I tried to obey when I was in bed under the covers. The other was: "Sleep tight, and don't let the bed bugs bite," an itchy bedtime thought indeed.

The unmarried daughter of the house, Aunt Lily, welcomed me the moment I arrived at the big stone house in Chestnut Hill, and always, the first thing, I went rushing up the sweeping front staircase to the landing where there was a tall chest of drawers. In a certain drawer, low enough for a child to reach, was a colorfully painted tin full of delicious crispy sand tarts, each with an almond and a sprinkling of crunchy cinnamon sugar grains on top. The bottom drawer was stacked with old-fashioned games and pop-up books. One was the scariest story in the world: "Old Mother Tabby Skins." I forced patient Aunt Lil to read it to me every single time I visited her in their dark Victorian house.

Old Mother Tabby Skins was a cat who dressed herself up as a nurse in cap, cloak, and white uniform. In her nurse disguise, she made a house call to a poor sick mouse. The illustrations were sinister, especially the moment when the little mouse-patient was gobbled up. I can still see Old Mother Tabby Skins smiling her treacherous cat smile with her long fangs, pink tongue, and the mouse's little tail dangling from the corner of her mouth! Shudder!

Aunt Lil devoted herself to church affairs and was a selfless worker for many worthy causes. Her sister, my aunt Charlotte Cheston, was a robust smiling lady, and both of them had been internationally ranked field hockey players when they were girls. They went out to the Pacific and beat the team from Fiji, thus becoming a family legend. All the Chestons, five sons and two daughters, grew up to be hard working, greatly respected, successful and cheerful.

My father was the oldest, and he told the story that when he was a freshman at the University of Pennsylvania, he came home on vacation, and noticed his mother was looking sort of frumpy in a baggy dress, unlike her usual trim self. He complained, "Mother you really must find a new dressmaker, your clothes don't fit you, they are much too loose." She had not confided in him, even though he was nineteen years old, that she was about to have her seventh child. He was horrified at the thought of his elderly parents "making" a baby.

Visiting my paternal grandparents the Chestons in Chestnut Hill was very different from the jolly times I had visiting Aunt Mae, my mother's sister, in her large mansion up the hill. She had a lovely kind face, a snorting laugh and a humorous approach to life. I didn't realize until I was a teenager that more often than not she was quite tipsy.

Actually, both my mother's sisters became alcoholics, something I never noticed or understood until I was past girlhood. It was never discussed. The affliction got worse as they grew older, or perhaps I grew old enough to comprehend it. Only now, as I write this, do I realize Daddy's insistence on self-discipline was one of the influences that may have kept my mother from joining her two sisters in their fate, because she too loved "a good time." However, she had great strength of character, and an optimistic frame of mind, which her sisters may have lacked as they grew older and lonely in their widowhood.

One thing my father could never succeed in persuading Mummy to do was to give up her beloved Parliament cigarettes. "Just like a damned one-armed paperhanger," he would rail at her, as she blissfully puffed away, holding her cigarette with one hand and writing with the other.

Sandy Run was boring in comparison with the convivial life my more emancipated school friends enjoyed in Chestnut Hill. I grew up mostly ignorant of art, culture, travel, languages, the Great Depression, and the looming threat of War. My cousin said years later: "We were brought up like peasants in the Tyrol." Nevertheless it was a happy and fortunate childhood except for that insulation from the larger world, and for a long time I didn't understand what I was missing.

# 9

## *Sex and Growing Up*

It was June, and I was about 12 years old, driving back from Camp Hill in the rumble seat of my mother's car after a long afternoon swimming and sunning. The dusk was permeated with the heavy sweetness of honeysuckle and summer, and as I breathed in the sensuous perfumed air, the first strong, mysterious stirrings and restless longings engulfed me. It was an awakening; unrequited, and unrecognized for the future power it would hold over me.

That same summer, I was sitting at my desk in my thin cotton pajamas, when our big English spaniel came up to me, and companionably stuck his cold nose hard into my crotch and gave it a delicate lick. I was blown away. A jolt traveled through my entire body and left me trembling and thrilled. There had never been anything like it in my life before, and I wanted more, but what? How? My Victorian upbringing strictly dictated that certain things like Sex and "female problems" were left unexplained, and never even mentioned. My mother never brought up the subject, and I guess I was too shy to talk about "it," even if I had known enough to ask. I never heard about "sex" (meaning the actual act) until just before I went to boarding school, and I had never seen my brothers or my father naked, or any other adult male for that matter.

And yet, on my own, when I was about seven, I found out a peculiar thing about boys. I was sent off to play with two male cousins, slightly younger than me. The older one, Paul, suddenly asked me: "Do you want to see us write our names in the sand?" With no further ado, he and his kid brother Henry unbuttoned their linen shorts. Each boy whipped out something that resembled a tiny pink hose, and they wrote their initials in jets of sparkling watery script. I was amazed! How did they do it? As the old saying goes, a good thing to bring on a picnic!

A few years later, during a family trip to Atlantic City, Maisie my oldest girl cousin hoarded enough extra coins for Minnie and me to slip into a special exhibit on the Steel Pier. COMPLETELY NUDE! EVERYTHING

REVEALED! SHOCKING REALISM! The bright posters lured and intrigued us. Behind a curtain was Jacob Epstein's gigantic statue of Adam. Now my cousins and I would find out the secret for sure! What a sad disappointment. Adam was there all right, but with his back to us, and a cunning system of mirrors rigged to show his front only above the navel. We left the exhibit poorer in cash and none the wiser about male anatomy.

My incredible ignorance of "the facts of Life" lasted into my early teen years. By then I had received plenty of twisted information from my friends who claimed vast knowledge on the forbidden subject; for example, that the mysterious art of making a baby had to take place in the doctor's office, mother and father on the operating table, with doctor and nurse in attendance. The only sexual instruction my mother had ever given me was: "Don't ever let a boy touch you, or kiss you on the lips." Kiss me? I couldn't imagine such an embarrassment. At the movies, I always squinched my eyes tight shut when the people on the screen started kissing.

My Aunt Mae, who was more lenient than my parents, sometimes arranged for us to go to Saturday afternoon matinees at a movie theater in Glenside, to see "selected short subjects" and the thrilling cowboy serials, all tantalizingly "continued next week." One Saturday when I was about ten, my older cousin and I were trying to find seats in the darkened movie house. We were about to sit down, when I saw something that made me poke her and whisper, "What's that?" A man in the seat nearest us was holding a giant cup of popcorn in his lap. Behind the popcorn in the darkness, I could see the outline of a long snake-like thing weaving back and forth. My cousin rushed me to a different part of the theater, saying "Don't look, don't look!" without explaining. I have a vivid picture of it in my mind to this day.

Another time when I was about thirteen I had an encounter with a boy I didn't like. Actually I hadn't heated up enough to "like" any boy at all. I just didn't get it, all this pairing off and having crushes. We were at an awful—for me—dancing class party called "The Friday Evening," held at the Philadelphia Cricket Club, in Chestnut Hill.

Everyone knew Bill was madly in love with my cousin Minnie, and he held her closely during a long dance before he came up to me, sweating hot-faced and red, to ask me to dance. Minnie, who was always solicitous about my backward sex life, probably ordered him to. I got through the dance somehow, aware of something strange in Bill's pants when he tried to press up against me. When the number was thankfully over, I whispered to one of my friends: "Bill has a huge roll of coins in his pocket. Why would he need to take all that money to dancing class?" They all howled with laughter, but didn't enlighten me. Later, I endured many jokes about "pocket change" from girls who knew how to arouse ardor in their boyfriends.

It seems impossible to forbid something without explaining or mentioning it, but this was how "sex" was handled, or rather avoided in those days, at least in my sheltered world. I had been taught that "going all the way" without marriage was a sin. This transgression carried a lasting brand of shame—the Scarlet Letter—but only for the girl, not the boy.

The honest terms used today for sexual anatomy and body functions were completely unknown to me. All my contemporaries commonly used euphemisms instead.

| | |
|---|---|
| _Disappear:_ | _as in "I need to disappear for a minute" (find the bathroom)_ |
| _Prink up:_ | _leave the room to apply lipstick, or comb hair (or pee)_ |
| _Powder my nose:_ | _need to pee_ |
| _Morning call:_ | _a bowel movement. Also: "Did you do your duty?"_ |
| _Number 1:_ | _pee_ |
| _Number 2:_ | _see "Morning Call." Also: "poop"_ |
| _The Curse_, also _Monthly Distress:_ | _menstrual period_ |
| _That Way:_ | _another reference to the Curse, as in "Don't ever go swimming when you are 'that way.'"_ |
| _Bosoms:_ | _breasts_ |
| _Thing:_ | _penis_ |
| _Place:_ | _the female nether region. Also known as Down There, as in "Don't forget to wash Down There."_ |
| _Sex:_ | _used only to distinguish between Male and Female, but never discussed, as in "Did she Have SEX?"_ |
| _First Base:_ | _kissing_ |
| _Second Base:_ | _touching the breasts_ |
| _Third Base:_ | _fiddling around "down there"_ |

*All The Way*, also
*Home Run*:          *the ultimate act (fast girls only)*

*God Dammit to Hell*: *a bad curse. We had never heard the "F" word, or the "S" word.*

Daddy was always strict with me. He was my personal house detective. After I started going to parties in my late teens, I was not allowed to sleep late, no matter what time I had gone to bed. He woke me before nine, noisily pushing open the door to my room, which was never locked, privacy for children and teens being unknown in our house. "Who do you think you are anyway, some kind of a princess? GET UP and have your breakfast!"

When I was finally allowed to go out with a boy unchaperoned, around age eighteen, my father mercilessly interrogated each prospective date: the would-be escort's full name, address, age, school, years of driving experience, and even the names of his parents and grandparents. All these questions were part of Daddy's third degree. If the boy was finally permitted to take me out for the evening, my father waited up for me to come home. As soon as he heard the car crunching on the gravel driveway, no matter what the hour, he was on hand to open the front door, dressed in his red flannel wrapper.

My unfortunate escort, having previously managed to hurdle the first barrier, would now be inspected for any unsteadiness, or the slightest whiff of alcoholic breath. Offered a glass of milk, and urged to discuss the party—with my father present, of course—the boy always declined that loaded invitation. The whole awful routine precluded even the remote chance of a good night kiss, or a tentative grope in the car. This kind of control would have taken place the summer of my "coming out" season. Only, I never came out officially, because it was still wartime, 1944.

I might as well have been in purdah, so carefully did my watchdog family eliminate any opportunities for sexual experimentation. By spring term at boarding school, two months shy of my eighteenth birthday, I was—I mean this—the only girl in the senior class except for my two best friends Joan B. and M.F.P. who had never been kissed.

On our one weekend away from school late in the spring term, at a classmate's coming-out party, I was having a great time dancing with everyone. Even though I didn't know any of the boys, I discovered I loved dancing, and was naturally good at it. To my happy surprise, I found myself suddenly popular. The dancing was held out on their lawn in a gala tent decorated with masses of colored balloons. Meyer Davis and his famous orchestra were playing all the catchy tunes of the day. In those days the girls and boys rarely knew each other, because of the war, and boarding school separateness. A barbarous dancing class type situation existed. The boys hung out in a stag line, smiling to each other with what we thought of as knowledgeable superiority, looking us over as though we were eligible fillies in the Saratoga sale ring. We girls danced by, trying not to appear too hopeful, especially when we were stuck for too long with an obvious drip.

But I was lucky. A handsome sailor in a white bell-bottom uniform cut in; he had no difficulty luring me away from the dance floor and into the library of the mansion. I was on the brink of my eighteenth birthday, and determined to break the kiss barrier. I wanted to report this rite of passage to my friends at school who had been teasing me unmercifully.

My heart thumped as the sailor closed in. At the last moment, dire parental warnings about the wages of sin echoed in my brain. On an impulse, I picked up a hoop of embroidery from the coffee table, and thrust it between the kiss and me. Off limits, sailor! His startled face broke right through the hoop, embroidery and all. The moment lost, the opportunity bungled, we made our embarrassed way back to the party, and that was that.

Later, while being driven back from the dance, another boy tried to make out with me in the back seat of the car, and I hated his sloppy wet attempt to put his tongue in my mouth. "You'll have to get an oyster knife if you want to open my mouth," I joked, thinking I was being funny. I just wasn't turned on, and after that turn off, I never saw him again.

Why didn't I rebel, or sneak around? Of course I was scared of repercussions, but more importantly I didn't want to disappoint my parents' faith in me. I had plenty of chances to experiment after I got to college and away from parental supervision, and eventually did my share of mild necking. All my life, my pheromones have been powerfully "out there," and I never had trouble attracting males (only trouble after they were hooked). But it really wasn't until I was nineteen, when I met my future husband, the charming and rakishly experienced Whitney Tower, that true sexual feelings began to heat up.

After my engagement was announced, in June of 1947, when I was a month short of my twenty-first birthday, my mother and father warned me that if anything happened—translation: pregnancy before the wedding—they would "never be able to hold up their heads again."

They insisted that we make an appointment with their elderly, dignified Episcopal minister, Dr. Nathaniel Groton, for pre-marital counseling, which Whitney and I assumed would be purely religious in nature. We were mystified when he warned us to be sure to make use of the "heavenly sphere," then astounded when we figured out he was pro birth control, and was recommending the use of a diaphragm. When my mother privately repeated this advice to my father, he was horrified. "Only prostitutes use those things!" he snorted, and objected strenuously when she insisted on escorting me to a new gynecologist for a "fitting." At last I visited the operating table of my early imaginings, with its scary steel stirrups, and embarrassing intrusive probing.

They spirited me across the border into Canada ostensibly for a wilderness fishing trip, in spite of the vociferous objections of my fiancé, and wouldn't allow me to see him until just before the wedding in September. Canada was my parents' idea of contraception.

The underlying reason I married so young was to try out that exotic still unfulfilled destination, "All The Way." At the time it seemed overwhelmingly more important than a college diploma, and I quit Bryn Mawr College after my junior year, an unimaginable decision today.

# 10

## *The Greatest Show On Earth*

One of the special treats my father arranged for me was the annual trip to The Ringling Brothers Barnum and Bailey Circus, truthfully advertised as the Greatest Show on Earth, with its three frenetic rings of simultaneous action, competing Death-Defying Acts, spider webs of ropes and rigging, wild horses, and cavorting comical clowns.

He always let me invite a friend, and we arrived early enough to walk the sawdust trail through the Reading Railroad Yards where the Big Top was pitched. A forest of poles held up an enormous tented dome of white canvas, with its colorful pennants streaming from the peaks, and everywhere the unforgettable circus smells of elephants, popcorn and lions.

The wide path to the main tent curved between the brightly painted cages of the menagerie. Snarling tigers paced endlessly behind their confining bars, and the elephants swayed and pulled gently at the heavy chains that each one wore attached to a hind leg. They reached out with their gray wrinkled trunks, hoping for a peanut handout, almost close enough to touch.

Vendors hawked their pink and blue bundles of cotton candy, hot dogs, soft drinks, whips, rubber swords, and ostrich plumes. Best of all, they sold tiny green turtles painted with flowers, baby alligators, and live lizards wearing little collars with chains connected to a pin, so that you could wear them home as lapel ornaments. The crowds were excited and good-natured, and we always came home with a special souvenir after the show.

The Sideshow was set up beyond the menagerie cages, and the "freaks"—that's what they called themselves—sat out in front of their own special tents, previewing the individual acts that were staged after the main performance, and for which you paid extra.

There sat the Fat Lady, overflowing the edges of her chair, dressed in a baby-doll costume that showed off her dimpled knees. ("She weighs more than four hundred pounds, and has been married five times," announced the barker); the Tattooed Man ("Tattooed over every inch of his body"); the Petrified Man ("Watch while we drive nails right into his legs!"); the Alligator-Skinned Woman (she later made headlines when she married the Tattooed Man); the Bearded Lady ("Yes, folks, she is 100% female"); the Sword and Flame Swallower; the Gentle Irish Giant (his souvenir ring could fit around my wrist); the Pinheads (who talked in high piping alien voices); the Snake Charmer (a sexy and scantily clad woman who allowed her python to take liberties); the Dog-Faced Boy, the Strong Man, the Giraffe-necked Women, the dwarves, and the famous midgets, General and Mrs. Tom Thumb (who were "married" during every main performance), and the rest of the gang making up the sideshow.

After so many annual visits, I felt as though I knew them personally, and they often held lively conversations with the crowd while they sold their autographed photos and trinkets. They didn't seem to mind being gawked at as it was their livelihood, and there was a definite camaraderie among them. They were part of the same circus family tradition as the headliners, like the phenomenal trapeze artists, the acrobats, the lion tamer and the clowns, and the amazing Flying Wallendas. These were a family of daredevils who formed a six man/woman acrobatic pyramid on the shoulders of one bicycle-rider, who wheeled them precariously forward and backward on the high wire, balancing all of them with a long swaying pole. There was no safety net.

I remember Unus the Great, clad in a somber black suit and top hat. He sat on top of a teetering stack of chairs, which became taller and more precarious as his act progressed. Each time his assistant tossed another chair to him, Unus would catch it, and add it to the stack under him, then climb atop this new chair to receive the next one, and the next. Then he was thrown a large ball, on which he balanced even more precariously at the top of the high stack of chairs. Finally, to the accompaniment of a menacing roll of the snare drum, he caught a slender black walking stick. He flipped himself up into a handstand on top of the cane, which in turn was balanced on top of the ball, on top of the stack of chairs. Then…slowly, slowly…he released one hand, and finally, supported himself on one single, straight forefinger.

"Unus, you're a fake, you've got a steel brace in your finger!" skeptics in the audience yelled. Easing himself down onto the top chair and casually tossing the ball to his assistant, he stared the audience down, and then—very disdainfully and theatrically—he bent and waggled the forefinger at them.

After long anticipation, near the end of the show, accompanied by great fanfare and hyperbolic praise from the Ringmaster, a man was shot out of the cannon. He looked noble but apprehensive in his white jump suit and silver Lindbergh-style helmet, as he let himself down into the huge muzzle of the cannon. The drums rolled, the tension built…until, with a flash of flame, a thunderous BANG and a puff of smoke, the "Human Projectile" flew across the entire ring, to land with triumphant, graceful bounces on a narrow black net.

Between the performances of the headliners, the clowns raced about chaotically, trying to put out the flames of a burning house with ineffective squirt guns, while a fat woman clown stood on the roof, clutching a squirming bundle in her arms and begging the clown firemen to *"Save my baby!"* The fire engine finally raced up, siren wailing, and the "lady" threw down the baby…that turned out to be a puppy, which scampered merrily off in its trailing nightgown!

The famous clown and car act never failed to bring laughs no matter how many times I saw it. A tiny car suddenly appears, speeding around the center ring, honking its horn noisily, and darting at the ringside roustabouts, its windows painted black so as not to reveal the secret inside. A policeman rushes into the ring, blowing his whistle, gesturing for the driver to halt and get out.

One by one from inside the tiny car, at least six clowns unfold themselves and go rushing away, as the policeman clown (usually a bandy-legged dwarf) threatens them with his nightstick. The last clown out of the car is Jack Earle, the actual "Gentle Giant" from the sideshow. The crowd cheers and laughs, sure that they have reached the amazing finale; after a pregnant pause, out of the car trots a live burro!

The wonderful circus band played familiar Sousa marches, peppy show tunes, and romantic waltzes for the graceful trapeze artists, as they somersaulted and crisscrossed on high in their beautiful costumes of spangles and tights. I remember the elegant way the ladies kicked off their high-heeled slippers, stepped out of their robes, hooked one leg around the rope, and with a nod and a radiant smile, were hoisted high to the top of the tent to pose on the staging platform while their brawny partners flipped the trapezes to and fro.

I never liked the conceited, peroxide-blond lion tamer, dressed in a leopard skin and boots, who forced his "wild" animals into undignified perches on stools, and made them jump through flaming hoops while he snapped a whip in front of their noses.

The beasts would snarl, and paw the air ineffectively, looking relieved when it was all over and they could slink back to their cages. Daddy told us that their claws had been pulled out, and that they were probably drugged.

The elephants were different. They seemed to enjoy performing, balancing on huge balls, sitting on chairs, doing headstands, and trotting smoothly and swiftly along, trunk to tail in the grand parade, with a little baby elephant bringing up the rear. Pretty girls in scanty, glittery costumes clung to the jeweled harness fastened behind each elephant's flapping ears, smiling bravely as they jolted along, waving to the applauding, cheering crowd.

One brave semi-naked girl allowed her favorite elephant to pick her up with his trunk and put her inside its huge mouth. She stayed there, drooped over on her back, her long hair trailing, trying to look cheerful as the parade wound on around the three rings.

After the main performance, Buffalo Bill's Wild West Show arrived. In the early days, a man dressed as the famous old Indian scout always opened the show. We thought him the real Buffalo Bill, with his trademark flowing grey locks and goatee, wearing his fringed and beaded buckskin jacket and carrying a long rifle. His horse bowed repeatedly to the crowd, and he waved his big hat, acknowledging the cheers.

Staying on to see it cost 75 cents extra, but Daddy loved the show because of the sharpshooters, the beautiful horses ridden by daredevil cowgirls, and the acrobatic riders who swooped low to the ground, plucking up two or three men in succession to ride behind them, while their ponies galloped around the ring at breakneck speed. He told me the reason the sharpshooters were able to powder their tiny targets to smithereens was that their pistols were loaded, not with bullets, but bird shot.

In another act, a piratical man came on, wearing tight pants and a ballooning silk shirt. He hurled gleaming knives at his patient and trusting target, a woman announced as his "wife" who leaned stiffly against the painted contour of her shape, while he outlined her body from head to toe, the last knife quivering between her upraised arm and her vulnerable and prominent bosom.

Next came the burly Australian cattleman, an expert with his sinister black bullwhip. The drivers were skilled with the whip, which they used back home in the Outback to nip flies off the backs of their oxen. After a theatrical warm-up, lashing and cracking his long bullwhip back and forth, snapping its braided tip with a sharp crack, he motioned another long-suffering female assistant to stand in front of him, twelve or fourteen feet away.

First, with a single whip crack, the cattleman clipped a lit cigarette from between the fair lady's lips, in a shower of tobacco and sparks. Next, he delicately teased a long silk handkerchief from the palpitating breast pocket of her silk blouse, taking at least five strokes of his lash to complete the task, while she stood there unflinching and smiling grimly, a brave and trusting woman. I hated to imagine their practice sessions!

After visiting the freaks, listening to their spiels and buying their postcards and souvenirs, came the tired drive home. It was the best of days, and the best of times. We were stuffed with hot dogs and peanuts, sticky from the cotton candy, and delighted with our toy whips and rubber knives, and those live turtles and chameleons. I still have the giant's silver ring.

I know that my father enjoyed it as much as we did. For that unforgettable outing each year, he and I were indeed "Children of all Ages."

# 11

## *Tally-Ho*

on the way to the Hunt - Mummy on "Miss Button"
Francie on "Measles"

D'ye ken John Peel with his coat so gay?
D'ye ken John Peel at the break of day?
D'ye ken John Peel when he's far far away
With his hounds and his horn in the morning?
Twas the sound of his horn brought me from my bed
And the cry of the hounds that he oft times led,

*For Peel's view-halloo would awake the dead.*
*Or the fox from his lair in the morning!*
—John Woodcock Graves (1832)

In the thirties we spent nearly every weekend at our farm in southeastern Penn-sylvania, near Unionville in Chester County. It was situated in lovely rolling coun-try, and the thick sod fields, substantial rail fences, and many wooded coverts made it ideal for fox hunting with Mr. Stewart's Cheshire Hounds.

My first memory of the hunt was in cubbing season, when the young hounds are first taken out to hunt with the members of the hunt, "the Field." In October the meets were scheduled in the early morning to avoid the heat of midday, and the hunt was much shorter than later on to allow for the relative unfitness of horse, hounds and riders. On this particular day, the meet was at our farm, and because I was too young to join in, I was awakened in the newly breaking dawn, bundled into a quilt, and taken out to hang onto a fence in back of our farmhouse from where I could view the action.

The crisp, cool morning mist was rising from the woods below the barn. The huntsman collected his hounds, blew stirring notes on the hunting horn, hallooed encouragingly, and the field cantered off. I watched them, two or three horses abreast, streaming fluidly over the line panels of the post and rail fence, close to where I was perching. I remember the clarion sound of the horn, the exciting thud of hooves, the spicy smell of the frosty turf, and the graceful power of horse and rider.

Later, at about the age of eight, I was allowed to follow along. Nothing could equal the pride and nervous thrill felt by a small girl trotting out to the meet on her fat piebald pony Measles.

On Opening Day, early in November, the field was dressed formally. My mother wore top hat and veil, an immaculate and intricately tied white stock pinned with a golden pin, and tightly fitting navy blue sidesaddle habit. Her shiny black boot, with one silver spur, just showed under the graceful skirt. A polished sandwich box was fastened to the side of the big padded saddle, the gleaming bit with its loose curb chain jingled, and her lovely bay mare, Miss Button, pranced lightly out on the bridle path to the meet, mane and tail braided for the occasion.

Grooming and tacking up the horses before the hunt required a large staff in those days, and dressing the riders was nearly as ritualized as dressing a matador for the *corrida*. At our farm there were two grooms and a stable boy to care for the horses; George Gates, the valet/butler took care of the men's boots, britches and coats, and Mummy's lady's maid from home helped to tie the linen stock, polished, brushed and outfitted her.

The hunt servants (whips and huntsman) and the Master wore velvet caps and scarlet coats, traditionally known as "pink" (named after Mr. Pink, the London tailor who was the first to make huntsmen's coats in this pattern). Long-standing hunt members were also permitted to wear pink on big days, like Thanksgiving. Shabby or informal garb was frowned upon, like tweed on a formal day, and rules were strictly enforced.

The two grooms accompanied us on the hunt. I always had fun and jokes with Bob Bennett, a handsome roguish Irishman who was assigned to watch over me and pick out easy two-rail panels for my pony to pop over safely. I think I must have proposed to him, because he promised faithfully to marry me when I grew up. I was crushed later on when I discovered that he had picked out a bride while on a vacation home to Ireland, and they eventually had eight children.

Bob was in charge of the tack room, which was a short distance from the barn. In its center, a wood stove heated water for washing off the saddles and bridles with sponges lathered in brown saddle soap. On the walls, the double bridles and snaffles, with their gleaming bits and curb chains, hung from rows of pegs—each one labeled with its horse's name. Checkered woolen blankets were folded neatly on tables, and English saddles were arranged on racks beneath their matching bridles. The tack room smelt of old leather, the reins and girths were soft and pliable and everything was spotless.

One awful day before the hunting season began, Daddy paid a surprise visit to the farm. This was during Prohibition, and Bob had been brewing corn liquor on the stove. Somehow he had to keep Daddy away, and so he invented ingenious reasons why they must inspect and discuss each and every hunter down in the big barn, and then take extra time to watch Harvey the hired man showing off his tricky milking routine, squirting jets of milk directly from the teat into an open-mouthed circle of meowing barn cats. After all that, and by the time he had visited the house and questioned the British couple who lived there year round, it had grown late and fortunately for Bob's sake, my father had to leave before checking out the tack room.

What a disaster! The brew had exploded, and every saddle and bridle was covered with a dripping layer of yellow whiskey mash. The smell of fermenting grain lingered for weeks. "Sure, and it is a new kind of saddle soap I've been tryin'," says Bob, not fooling wise old Jack Totham the head groom, who nevertheless did not give him away. "A near thing, praise be to God!" Bob told me later. "Your father would not have been pleased!"

Mr. and Mrs. Gates took care of our rambling farmhouse, Cheshire Lodge, which was painted a lovely dark rose color. "Gates," as they always called him, had been shell-shocked in World War I, and when he passed the dishes at meals, the plates rattled as if we were in an earthquake. His wife Cecily was an admirable cook, and her lemon-curd tartlets were as light as whispers. Gates loved complicated dart contests, and I used to play pub-style games with him in their sitting room off the kitchen.

The head groom John Totham was a bandy-legged, jockey-sized Cockney and a fine horseman. He looked out for my mother and father, opened gates, and held the horse for my mother when she dismounted. His wife, always "Mrs. Totham" to us, had suffered ~~a stroke~~ and her good countrywoman's face was all lopsided. She had a daughter Frances Ivy, who had a walleye that rolled disconcertingly outward from her nose. I often played with Frances Ivy although she was younger than me. Despite her stroke, Mrs. Totham made the best pies and candied apples I ever tasted and always welcomed me into their apartment at the back of the house.

*[margin note: Bell's Palsey]*

The arrival at the Opening Meet was thrilling. The field, as many as fifty on a big day, were meticulously turned out, exchanging greetings and looking critically or admiringly at each others' mounts. The male members of the hunt wearing their pink coats, sneaked nips from flasks strapped to their saddles, and their horses—fine, fit thoroughbreds—ready to explode, were sidestepping, pawing and farting in their impatience to be off.

Fox hunting hounds are always counted in pairs, known as a couple. Six hounds are called "three couple." Two hounds are "one couple of hounds."

In Mr. Stewart's pack, huge black, tan and white English-bred fox hounds milled around the legendary huntsman, Charley Smith, their sterns (tails) held high and waving, waiting impatiently for the signal to move off. When the notes from his golden horn echoed over the lovely autumn countryside, the whips gave a whoop, a cacophony of tongue sounded from the pack, and we were off. With luck, when the fox was started from a covert, one might glimpse his red coat reflecting the bright sunlight, usually running far ahead of the hounds.

The cry *"Tally-Ho!"* resounded, the horn called *"Gone Away,"* the horses plunged into their gallop and suddenly one small rider tightened her grip, shortened the reins, and felt a surge of confidence replacing nervous apprehension. I was a foxhunter!

During a run, when the blood is up, and the horses pound along together, their ears pricked, their riders steadying them for the looming fence, all fear vanishes. No fence is too high, no gully too steep. I felt invulnerable, swept along by the excitement of the chase.

There have been many legendary runs made by the Cheshire Hounds. Once, after crossing the Brandywine Creek three times, the hounds finally checked at the amusement park at Lenape, after a five-hour and twenty-minute run that had actually taken them under the roller coaster, where the clever fox made good his escape.

This was a record day. Normally the hunt would stop for lunch to rest hounds, horses and riders, and allow a change of mount. Sometimes a rendezvous was arranged, and a sort of soup kitchen set up in a sheltered spot. Once I thought it would be nice to visit the hounds during lunch, and I walked over to give them part of my sandwich. One of the whips scooped me up onto his saddle. Those big hounds were as tall as I was, and might easily have swallowed the sandwich with my hand attached.

Another time, in my eagerness to be in the forefront, I followed the Master, Mr. Stewart, as he rode off alone after the lunch stop. Finally, as we entered a nearby wood, with me close at his heels, he turned and said, "Frances, do you mind going back, I have to get off my horse here!" It was one of the most embarrassing moments in my early hunting career! It did, however, reinforce the advice that it was important to empty your bladder before starting off, as this precaution prevented more complicated internal damage in case of a fall.

There was always a risk of serious accidents out hunting; in fact, my mother cracked a vertebra in her neck when her horse stepped in a gopher hole, and turned over. This accident was much dreaded by ladies mounted on sidesaddles, because they often were unable to be thrown clear. Foxhunters traditionally took the risk of accidents as part of the game. They called it being a bit "bunged up" if they happened to break a collarbone or arm, and the diehards started hunting again as soon as it was practical. I knew one 70-year-old lady who was so wired together that she had to have a special sidesaddle made, so she could hook her left leg over the pommel instead of the right.

I still have the fox's pad, presented to me "On the occasion of being blooded," dated 1935, when I was nine. Custom dictated that the Master dipped the fox brush in the fresh gore, and painted the recipient's cheeks, like the war paint on an Indian. I came home proudly wearing the swipes of dried blood that proved I had been in at my first kill. I remember how pleased my mother and father were...after they were reassured it was the fox's blood, not my own!

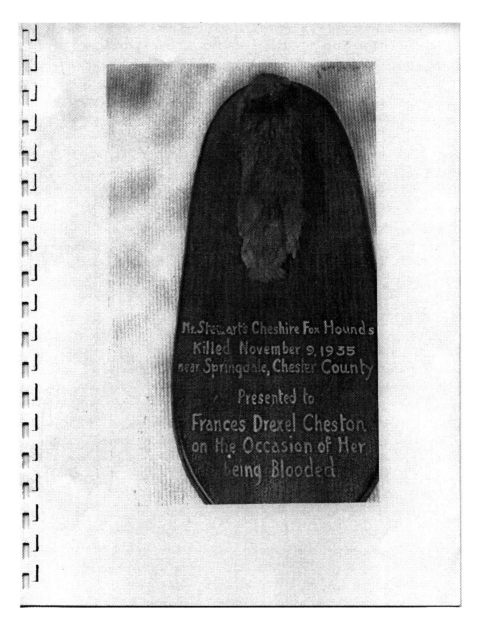

The wild chase, the fox's trickery, the baying of the hounds, the encouraging call of the horn, the great sport of flying over fences and galloping over the hills, the camaraderie and good sportsmanship of the riders, the ability of fine thoroughbreds, the skill of the huntsman, whips and the Master, and the triumph of surviving sometimes nasty weather and dangerous fences, all these things made for great sport. And more times than not, Reynard the Fox outsmarted huntsmen, horses and hounds.

After the holiday hunts, the grownups were invited to elaborate teas called "breakfasts" in the different houses belonging to the members of the hunt. Formal buffets were laid out on long mahogany dining room tables, loaded with delectable choices of hams and biscuits, curries, fricassees and pastries, and sometimes Maryland oysters on the half shell. There were footmen and butlers in attendance. The beautiful silver tea services were presided over by the ladies of the house, and later, fine whiskeys flowed as ruddy-faced men and women laughed and bantered about the events of the day's sport.

As for me, I loved hanging out in the warm barn after the long weary hack home from the hunt with the grooms. It would be growing dark outside, and the electric lights made the deep straw in the box stalls glow like Rumplestiltskin's gold.

The grooms hissed soothingly and kept up a steady patter of comforting talk while they washed and sponged off each hunter with steaming buckets of water. Their manes and tails were combed out and brushed, and their legs wrapped with flannel bandages that smelt pungently of Absorbine Jr. liniment.

Then, their coats were rubbed down with soft dry cloths, and their hooves examined carefully, especially the "frog"(the soft under section of the hoof). Any pebble or clod of dirt caught in a horse's frog was carefully removed with a hoof-pick. My job was painting each hoof with oil from a battered tin, until it gleamed. Then the warm checked blankets were buckled on, and each horse was led to his stall where a delicious smelling bucket of warm bran mash awaited.

The odors of fresh pungent hay, grainy steamy mash, the soft breath of clean warm horses, and the sounds of satisfied crunching made the evening barn a place of magic and cozy contentment.

Then it was a hot tub, an early supper, and a soft bed where I dreamed of great doings...where the heroic pony Measles and I were first at the kill, or first to view the fox, or first over a three-rail fence, and singled out and complimented by the Master for a particularly magnificent performance.

**Happy Dreams    Brave Dreams**

# 12

## *Being Young in Dark Harbor*

Dark Harbor, Islesboro, Maine

Every July we traveled to our summer place on the island of Islesboro, riding on the Bar Harbor Express from Philadelphia to Rockland, Maine. Our household took up almost an entire car, what with the steamer trunks, the wicker hampers full of linen and silver, many servants, Mummy and Daddy, brothers George and Antelo, sister Sydney, the dogs, Margaret and me.

The track was rough and the train slow as it approached the station. There everyone was loaded into the taxis that took us onto the wharf, and the steamboat *Pemaquid*, for the one-hour crossing of Penobscot Bay to the pier on Islesboro Island, near Dark Harbor. I always felt queasy on the swaying lurching train, and seasick on the rolling steamboat, as much from the excitement of actually starting the summer holiday as the motion.

Mr. Hale, a taciturn angular man, met us with buckboard and surrey, and drove us the mile and a half on the dirt road to our "cottage." The dear old house welcomed us with its bright flowers, and salty sea smell, and the enchanted summer began. I dashed about taking an instant inventory of the shelves and bureaus that reassuringly revealed the same games and books and decks of cards, with the jokers still substituting for missing face cards, the mildewed Currier and Ives prints on the walls, the faded chintz and the colorful old hooked rugs. The stuffed baby seal remained at his post by the hall fireplace, and the ancient life preservers still hung from their hooks on the cellar stairs.

The house has remained virtually unchanged since my childhood, and is still shared harmoniously by our extended family. It was built in 1915, and, conforming to my mother's wishes, "as close to the water as possible." Our view is to the west, over the harbor. The summer sunsets, with the blue undulating Camden Hills as a backdrop, are flamed with color: saffron, scarlet, and turquoise. We can hear the clanging of the bell buoy at the harbor entrance, and see the intermittent sweeping beam of Gilkey's lighthouse behind the ferry landing. The deep foghorn groans through foggy days and nights, and its warning carries on through the years in my memory.

In the early 1930's there were no cars belonging to "summer people" on the thirteen mile-long island of Islesboro, and there were no paved roads. In 1933, when automobiles were finally allowed on the island by the local town government, the first cars traveled the five miles across the bay aboard a scow, waves slopping over their wheels, windshields drenched with spray, and were driven off onto a wooden ramp up the rocky beach.

All the years before that time, the grownups went to their dinners and luncheons and golf by boat, Chris-Crafts and power launches, or, if the weather was too bad, by hired surrey from one of the livery stables. The kids walked to their friends' houses, or rode their bikes.

There had been a near war between the summer people and the "natives" over the car question. Many of the island people wanted the convenience of the automobile and the tractor, but the rich summer visitors wanted to keep things quaint and old-fashioned. The livery stable owners wanted to keep the cars out, and the horses, which were their livelihood, in. But once the ban against autos was lifted, they quickly adapted, and converted their stables to garages and repair shops. One of them, Pendleton's Livery Stable morphed into the successful Pendleton's Yacht Yard. Some of the summer people were so incensed when cars were finally allowed that they threatened to sell their houses, and one irate owner said she would burn down her house rather than see the horses displaced.

The pure enjoyment of this island has changed very little for kids during the last seventy-five years. Of course, outboard boats are faster now than my first 1.5-horsepower, which I had inherited from my brother George. The engine was precariously fastened to the stern of a modified Old Town canoe, which made it terribly tippy, but still faster than most. All my friends were jealous of me when we met up in the bay for our daily zooms.

Children still walk and bicycle to Mr. Randlett's store (now the Dark Harbor Shop) where all ages meet for afternoon ice cream cones, gossip, and plans for tomorrow. Old Mr. Randlett, in those days, knew all the kids and their fathers and mothers and grandparents. Sometimes, when there wasn't a big crowd, he would let us go behind the counter and build our own horrendous ice cream sundae concoctions, overflowing with chocolate sauce, chopped nuts and strawberry syrup. No money ever changed hands; he always knew which parents to charge. The ice cream shop still exists, run by genial Billy Warren in the same tradition as Mr. Randlett. (Last year, my grandson crowed to me: "I just love it here in Dark Harbor: everyone knows me, and everything is free!")

In my youth, our friends gathered in mid morning at the big Dark Harbor tidal basin, which was our swimming pool. We changed in the rickety bathhouses and ran down to belly-flop off the float, and whiz down the long slide into the freezing water.

The older girls posed self-consciously in their new Esther Williams-type, white sharkskin swimsuits, and bathing caps topped off with fashionable rubber flowers. They only half-resisted with laughing shrieks when the boys tried, and usually succeeded, in pushing them off the float.

All the Dark Harbor summer families on the southern end of the island knew each other, but we rarely ever explored beyond the narrows to North Islesboro. The old settlements were widely separated, so that before the coming of cars, there were five post offices and three schools to accommodate the clusters of little villages, with their white-painted, wooden cape houses and small subsistence farms. Much of the land was cleared for sheep pasture, but now it is covered in thick spruce forest. Fishing was always the main source of livelihood and many islanders still go lobstering today, their sturdy powerboats replacing the lovely old wooden friendship sloops.

In the 19th century, the Pendleton family owned a large and profitable fleet of home-built coastal trading schooners; the imposing houses built by their captains still exist. Carpentry and boat building were then, and still are today, ubiquitous and important skills for island dwellers. There were three landings for the steamboats that brought mail and supplies and transported passengers to Castine, Belfast and Rockland on the mainland. Ice was harvested from Meadow Pond. In Maine, the ice trade was immensely profitable; winter ice was shipped from Port Clyde as far south as Brazil to cool the Christmas drinks.

Once each summer, we four cousins and our mothers and fathers were driven in a buckboard all the way up to our great-uncle George Drexel's substantial cottage Gripsholm, on the bluff at Sabbathday Harbor, a distance of some nine miles. It was a painfully formal Sunday lunch, and we dreaded it. Aunt Mary was an invalid, and always received us reclining on a sofa, draped in floaty chiffon and white cashmere scarves. Kissing her was mandatory, like kissing a marshmallow, so powdery and soft were her cheeks.

Uncle George was always a lover of the sea, and he kept his beautiful 275-foot yacht *Alcedo* moored in the cove near his big boathouse (until it was sunk in World War I). Once a passing lobsterman's boat happened to break down nearby. Spotting an old geezer in khaki shirt and oil-stained trousers, the fisherman asked for assistance. The two men worked together companionably—and probably profanely—and got the cranky engine going again. The lobsterman said thanks and handed over a five-cent tip, never suspecting that he was offering a nickel to our millionaire great-uncle George Drexel and, you guessed it: Uncle George accepted the nickel.

The sounds of summer and freedom are still typified by the slap, flap, stamp, of sneakers, bare feet, and flip-flops, running down the long vibrating docks and bouncing gangways to the floats; kids yelling back and forth; the splash of oars; the slatting of sails being hoisted; and the roar of outboards speeding off to freedom from adult supervision.

In those days we wore our ribbed, khaki-colored Neversinks (now grandiosely labeled *Personal Flotation Devices*) all day long, their ties haphazardly fastened. I was told I surprised some guests by even wearing mine to breakfast. We were constantly in, or on, the blue-green waters of the bay; fishing, sailing, racing our 12 1/2 foot Herreshoff sailboats, driving the outboards, rowing, and swimming off the rocky beach or float.

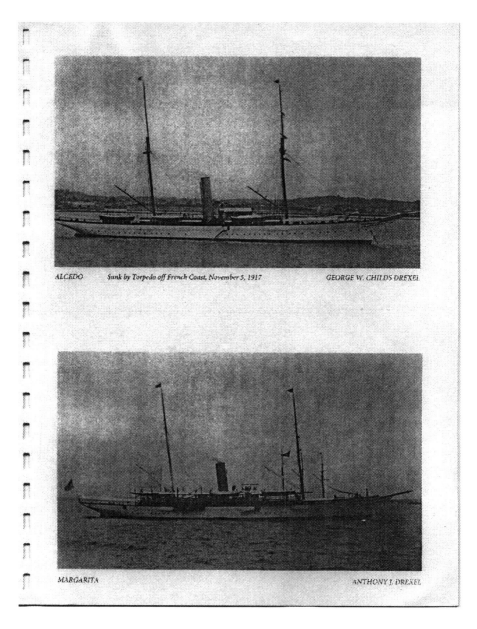

ALCEDO    Sunk by Torpedo off French Coast, November 5, 1917    GEORGE W. CHILDS DREXEL

MARGARITA                                        ANTHONY J. DREXEL

Flounder lines, with the twine wound around wooden frames, were always at the ready. I was an early expert at spotting clams' squirt-holes on our pebbly beach, and gunnysacks of steamer clams for bait were hung over the side of the float. I would smash a clam on the wooden cleat, peel off the skin from its muscle and head, because I thought that the flounder—like children—wouldn't like skin, and thread it onto the hook. Long experience taught that a dexterous crab could easily steal the soft stomach.

The technique was to let the sinker touch bottom, haul up six inches so that the bait just cleared, and fish the line up and down, up and down. At the slightest nibble, you jerk the line, pull it up hand over hand, and here comes your flounder, flipping and flapping until he joins his mates in the bucket. They were fat from the rich gleanings off our sewer line. Sometimes we caught ugly spiny sculpins, or horrid skates with their humanoid pink lips, and overboard they went. I caught so many flounder that the cook threatened to quit and go back to Philadelphia if she had to cook another one. (Now, sixty years later, the flounder are all gone from the bay.)

Those sweet summer days, with the tide coming in, and good friends competing for the most, the biggest, or the nastiest fish were perfection.

Twice a week we kids raced the twelve-footers, aided in my case by a "Captain": Bernie Young, my parents' boatman. He wasn't a very good sailor, being a lobsterman by trade, and we never did very well, but every minute was exciting…especially the daredevil starts, with the little boats slashing toward the line and howls of "Right of way!" "Starboard tack!" and "Protest!" We took our racing extremely seriously, and tried our utmost to concentrate, and obey the racing rules.

After the race, one or another of the parents laid on delicious teas. On cold foggy days, when we were chilled and soaking wet from spray, hot sweet tea and cozy fires were unsurpassed pleasures. I especially remember the teas at Mr. and Mrs. Wolcott Blair's house next door, because they had a fancy New York cook, and sometimes the beautifully frosted cakes were sent up on the train from Robert Day Dean's confectionary store in New York City. It seemed to me that we were always hungry. Then, home to a hot soak in a deep old claw-footed, cast-iron tub, the disappointment of an unsuccessful race forgotten, and another day of summer happiness ahead.

The Blairs' son Watson was just my age, and we played and sailed together right into our teens. Once when we were about twelve, rolling around on our lawn, my mother called me over to the porch and hissed, "Frances, you are too old to wrestle with Waddy after Sunday lunch in front of all the guests." It hadn't occurred to me, or Watson, that we were different sexes or that grownups might think of other explanations when they saw a boy and girl wrestling.

My friends and cousins and I climbed rocks, explored the beaches, assembled precarious rafts out of old logs, picked berries, played baseball, organized treasure hunts, played kick-the-can, and held our own day picnics. The evening picnics with all ages were the best fun. There were campfires on the beach, and lots of harmonizing to the old songs like "Casey Jones," "She'll be Coming Round the Mountain" and "Clementine." My friend Lucy Aldrich was famous for her raucous rendition of

> *The waiter bellowed down the hall, you get no bread with one meatball.*
> *One meatball! One meatball, you get no bread with one meatball.*

When it was time to go home we giggled at the grownups trying to maneuver up the rocks a bit off balance due to too many martinis. We never noticed the mosquitoes, and the camaraderie of those picnics bonded us summer families over all the years and down through the generations.

On foggy days the gang met for games of sardines, poker, twenty-one, Monopoly, and all sorts of card tricks. We played in our big attic, or stayed alone, absorbed in wonderful books. On good days we went for long explorations on the rocky beaches, leaping from rock to rock, picking mussels at low tide and wading in the cold shallows, looking for crabs and treasures. On shore there were luscious wild raspberries and blackberries to pick.

When we became teenagers, there were organized tennis clinics presided over by an imposing instructor, Mr. Klingeman, who was always impeccably attired in cream-colored flannel trousers and a V-necked cable-stitched sweater. There were golf lessons from the longtime pro, George Ira Dodge: a thin, patient man whose practical instruction created lifelong lovers of the game, and more than a few champions, like my childhood friend, Laura Leonard Ault who was many times club champion of the highly competitive Piping Rock Club on Long Island.

The only doctor we had for years was Dr. Harness, who drove around in his flivver making house calls, usually timing his visits so as to stay on to cadge a meal or a cocktail. I know he liked many of the ladies of the house, and they in turn enjoyed his company. In those days the younger husbands worked in their offices for the greater part of the summer, while the women and children enjoyed the long vacation days of summer. Often the families hired tutors for their sons—handsome young college men who were supposed to teach them golf, sailing, tennis and schoolwork. They sometimes escorted the mothers to parties, and the late nights that ensued often resulted in tutors oversleeping, and lesson hours curtailed, much to the joy of the boys. Tutors had the opportunity for romances with the young girls of the households, some even leading to marriage. All in all, it was an enviable summer job.

I spent many hours in the woodshed learning knots and macramé from Captain Young, and at low tide I would sometimes row out with him to watch as he scooped scallops from the harbor's bottom with a long-handled fish net. When he had captured four or five, he deftly cut the shells apart and slurped the still pulsing muscle. These scallops also lived near the end of our sewer line, but Bernie never seemed the worse for his raw snacks, and fortunately, I was too squeamish to try one. The circle of beady "eyes" around the edge of their shells fascinated me, especially when he told me that they shone in the dark. They clapped their lovely pink-ribbed shell halves together, and moved backwards in the watery bilges.

In those days, summer was a time for welcome relaxation from winter rules, except for the always-looming shadow of Summer Reading. No matter how pleasurable the books were that I chose for myself, the school's assignments seemed to inflict a sort of paralysis, which prevented me from opening the cover. Reading them was put off until the last possible moment after endless arguments and procrastination. The other downer was lessons. Mr. Hale, the livery stable proprietor, taught Math and Latin to many recalcitrant, inattentive students who didn't have their own tutors; it was lucky he was such a patient gentleman.

However, visiting the musty fusty library was a greatly anticipated treat. It was located above the Dark Harbor post office, and open only on Wednesday and Saturday. The books were mostly unreadable gray-backed Victorian novels that made you sneeze when you opened their dusty covers, but I always found a few good ones to take home. The expedition was well worth the walk to the village, because then I could walk around the corner and browse the stock at Peg's Gift Shop—items that never changed year in or year out.

Peg—Mrs. Earle—was a craggy-faced, corseted lady, who always wore a heavy hairnet over hair so tightly marcelled that a stiff breeze would not have mussed a curl. She was short on conversation and shorter on smiles, at least with the pesky, nosy kids who couldn't resist picking up the merchandise, and who never bought anything except on someone's birthday.

She sat in her rocker at the back of the store, near an electric heater that was turned on no matter what the weather, keeping a watchful eye peeled as we picked up and put down the little toy tomahawks, red metal lobsters attached to mailing tags, and balsam pillows of all sizes, with pictures of Indians paddling birch bark canoes, and "I Pine Fir Yew and Balsam Too" stenciled on their covers.

The post office next door held row on row of bronze, glass-fronted boxes, which one opened by twisting a pointer on an alphabet-coded dial. Spotting a letter in our box behind the glass was as exciting as finding a treasure, even though it was almost never for me.

Mrs. Ivy Babbidge was the serious postmistress, whom everyone called "Eye." I'm not sure if it was just short for "Ivy" or because it was on account of her prominent rolling walleye, hugely and scarily magnified by her wire-rimmed pince-nez.

Mrs. Philbrick operated the telephone switchboard in an old building farther up the road. She knew everyone on the island, and connected and disconnected the calls with the long rubber snakes that plugged into the appropriate holes in the switchboard. Our telephone was on the wall in the "cloak room" (hall closet). It was mounted on a long brown wooden box, and I had to stand on tiptoe to reach the mouthpiece, cranking the handle twice to ring up the operator. Mrs. Philbrick always answered promptly—"Mornin' Frances, number please." "Can I have the Aldriches please?" She listened in to many of the calls and knew what was going on that day, so she would be apt to say, "If you want Liberty, she ain't to home; she's over to Leonard's," and connect you there.

A little beyond the telephone office was Mrs. Hale's laundry, in the old wooden building that had once been a one-room schoolhouse. Mrs. Hale toiled away every day, tubs steaming and irons sizzling. In those days almost all the sheets and pillowcases were real linen. Somehow she never mixed them up, being an expert at deciphering and remembering complicated monograms. She was a famous storyteller in her inimitable Down East accent, and had a wealth of tales about that peculiar race, the summer folk.

One of her favorites involved the discomfiture of a new boy hired by her husband to deliver packages. Among the stops on the delivery schedule that day were families named the Birds, the Cranes and the Swans. The poor boy came back to the barn, mission unfulfilled: "I can't figure out which cottage is which with all them damn crazy summer people with them bird names!"

After work, Mrs. Hale loved to sit on her front porch, so densely screened by trumpet vine that she could see out, but no one could see in. There she would tell her stories, lubricated by judicious nips of blackberry cordial. She baked wonderful cakes for the golf teas, her specialty being a four-layer coconut masterpiece, so gooey that you had to have a bath after eating it.

Looking out my bedroom window on the annual Last Day before leaving for home, I can remember the overwhelming sadness of the end of vacation. Friends had been disappearing one by one, and those staying on a few days more were subjects of great envy. "Why do we have to go home? Why? Why?" The seagulls' clamor brought on waves of nostalgia and tears, and the long stretch of months before our return seemed unbearable.

What has happened to the endless summers of our youth? Today, summer jobs are sought for everyone over fourteen; greatly curtailed vacations for all the working mother and fathers; soccer camp, hockey camp, foreign-language camp, summer school, and educational trips abroad take up most of the holidays. Leisure has been replaced by compulsive activity. Admitting to doing "nothing" incurs a monumental guilt trip.

But happily for me, eighty years later, and still summering in my old family house, there are the same quarrelsome seagulls; the same enduring rocks, stony beaches, and green-blue sea; the fog and sun and splash of salt. Best of all, many of my original friends, now with their own children and grandchildren, return to this place, the well-loved Islesboro Island of our childhood, which we revisit year after year, like migrating seabirds...always coming home.

# 13

## *Overnight to South Carolina*

Every evening we could hear the long wailing whistle of the Black Diamond, warning of its approach to the crossing near our house in Whitemarsh, Pennsylvania. Sometimes I would stand by the edge of Sandy Run Creek and look up at the freight cars silhouetted against the western sky as they rattled over the high trestle bridge. The setting sun beamed between the wheels, the steamy smoke smelt of cinders, and the earth trembled under my shoes.

The engineer, wearing his jaunty black and white striped railroad cap, piloted his mighty locomotive with one hand, his elbow resting casually on the ledge of the cab. I would wave, and he'd grin, and wave back. One day he blew two more blasts on the whistle, just for me. I wished with all my heart that I could go with him. At that time, in the early 1930's, I thought every train, even the freights, went to Maine or to South Carolina, the two places to which my family traveled regularly.

The day after Christmas, we always headed south to Friendfield, my family's duck and quail shooting plantation, and every year my anticipation had built up to a fit of the jitters by the time the day of departure finally arrived. My mother, father, Marg and our two shivering dogs waited next to the heaps of bags on a gritty, cold platform of Philadelphia's 30th Street Station. The train always seemed to be late.

At last the brilliant searchlight flicked back and forth far down the track, and the sonorous announcement boomed and echoed through the station: "The Palmetto, arriving on Track 2. Train for Wilmington! Baltimore! Washington! Richmond! And points south! ALLLL ABOARRRRRRD!"

The long train, its brakes hissing and steaming, and its bell clanging, drew past the clumps of waiting passengers. White-jacketed porters leaned far out, to welcome them, and assist the redcaps with the baggage. We hurried to find the right rooms—Drawing Room A and Compartment B. No sooner were we settled than the train eased out of the station, and we were on our way at last! Train travel in those days was wonderful fun for children, completely different from being a passive, buckled up captive in an airplane. There was so much to do and observe.

Our compartment—containing my nurse and me, and Duggie, my Scottie—connected with the drawing room where my parents were ensconced with Trigger, their huge smelly springer spaniel, stacks of Louis Vuitton luggage, and English shotguns in polished leather cases. The redcaps had piled all the duffels and extra bags in the vestibule between the cars. No one ever worried about theft on the overnight trip.

One thing that did worry me, though, was what would happen if my dog made a "mistake" on the dark green carpet. I was certain that the all-powerful Conductor would have me thrown off the train—a fate too awful to contemplate. I imagined how terrible it would be for a seven-year-old in blue flannel pajamas to be left behind on some cold windy platform, and I dreaded the conductor's buzz at the door. He'd check the folder of tickets, punch them efficiently, hand the copies off to his sidekick, and then glare enigmatically at the dog. What was he thinking?

So, I used to get off at Wilmington, the next stop, and drag my poor dog by his unaccustomed leash, his toenails scraping on the inhospitable cement, and implore him to go. He never would, although he encouraged me with interminable, prolonged, disdainful sniffs. He was accustomed to grass and bushes, and he clearly had made up his stubborn Scottie mind that railroad platforms were not for that purpose. I feared his delaying tactics would cause us to miss the train, and I had to run to get on board, filled with misgivings, mission unaccomplished. Somehow he always lasted until morning, in spite of my anxiety.

I loved our cozy tan-painted room with its varnished trim, and the green plush seats with snowy linen antimacassars buttoned to their backs, but once the bags were stowed, and the dogs admonished to "Be Good!" I couldn't wait to rush out into the swaying passageway.

All the porters on the Pullman trains were "colored" men. I later learned that they had their own trade union, and received better wages (and tips) than many other workingmen, black or white, of the Depression era.

Following the signs that read DINING CAR IN THE REAR, I'd run way ahead of Marg, bouncing off the walls of the corridors, exaggerating the jerkiness of the train on purpose. It was hard to push open the balky handles of the doors. I would skip daringly across the shifting plates between the cars, like Eliza crossing the ice in *Uncle Tom's Cabin*, engulfed by the train's scary, deafening rattle and the cold cindery wind, until the safety of the next car was gained.

It was fun to peek into other people's compartments on the way. Red-faced tweedy gentlemen were swirling clear chunks of ice in tall whiskey glasses, and their wives—blue-haired and stiffly corseted—were already playing cards or drinking cocktails poured from their own frosted silver shakers. It was during Prohibition, but I was unaware they were breaking any laws. In those days, everyone dressed formally for train travel, the gentlemen wearing three-piece suits and ties, and the ladies sporting hats and traveling suits with jeweled lapel pins and pearls.

Some of them had children, whom I examined suspiciously and who looked just as strange to me as I must have to them. I used to pray that my family wouldn't know any of them, for fear we would have to be introduced, but unfortunately they usually did. The people in the Pullmans in those days constituted sort of a club; some who were going to shoot in South Carolina and Georgia, and the more richly-dressed Others, who were going on down to Palm Beach. I never wondered why my family knew so many of the other passengers, and it never crossed my mind that we were in any way privileged.

After the drawing room and then the compartments, came the "sections" in the regular Pullman car. To transform it into a sleeper, the porter would pull out the seats and fit them together, haul down the upper and make up the berths. Each individual section was then partitioned off from the aisle by two green curtains of a heavy impenetrable baize material, which the occupant, once safely inside, buttoned tightly together. When big people attempted to undress in their berths, the curtains bulged and billowed alarmingly, and it was tempting to give the bulge a fast slap or pinch while dashing by.

I lurched through the coaches, where whole families would be preparing for the long night of sitting up. Babies slept in their mothers' laps, and weary older folk stared out the window. Messy newspapers were strewn under the seats and the smell of orange peel and fried chicken pervaded the atmosphere. The older kids stared at me guardedly. I knew I looked alien in my gray flannel skirt and Buster Brown oxfords, as I trotted through on my way to the dining car.

The club car was filled with noisy men playing cards; I always ran as fast as possible through the smoke and sour, heavy smell of liquor. The first part of the diner was the corridor by the galley, and I joined the line of people in its passageway who were waiting to be seated by the steward. I looked out the window at the row houses edging the tracks. They were so close as we rattled by that I could spy right into their kitchens, and even see the wallpaper patterns. I thought about those children listening to their favorite radio programs and doing their homework. It was like inventing families for a dollhouse.

As soon as the steward showed us to the table, the waiter dexterously arranged a full complement of heavy silver flatware beside each place, selecting them individually from a pile underneath the big window. There was always a long-stemmed rose or carnation jiggling in the brightly polished bud vase on every table. The linen napkins were heavily starched and immaculately folded.

It made me feel important to write my own order. The waiter would smile patiently, as if he had all the time in the world, balancing there in his ankle-length white apron as I painstakingly printed out each choice. He studied it with care and then ripped off the first sheet, leaving the carbon for the important head steward to add up with great flourishes of his pencil, when it came time for my father to pay.

The cooks and waiters on the Pullman trains were always "colored," but in those days the steward was a white man. I noticed that the shoulders of his blue serge uniform were sprinkled with dandruff, and he seemed preoccupied and not very kind to the jolly waiters. When he made change, he peeled the singles off a fat roll of bills, and set down each coin with a little thump on a small silver tray.

The perspiring cooks turned out a variety of delicious dishes from the crowded little kitchen. They wore starched white tunics and tall chef's hats, and did all the cooking to order on a sizzling coal-burning range. On the return trip north, some hunters even gave them their own quail or ducks to cook.

The waiter loaded the dinners onto a huge tin tray that he balanced on the upturned palm of one hand, and made his way back to the table, swaying gracefully with the roll and lurch of the train.

Each thick plate was placed precisely in front of the diner, and then he removed its heavy chrome dome with a flourish. He always remembered who had ordered what, and the dinner arrived in jig time; choices of soup, fried chicken, grilled steak, or fried fish. Dessert was flaky crusted apple or cherry pie à la mode, or vanilla ice cream with hot chocolate sauce, served in frosty chrome compotes. Afterwards, you were given silver-chrome finger bowls lined with fluted paper.

And all the while you were dining, the changing scene scrolled by. Towns, bridges, rivers, factories, houses; passing images, seen and recorded through the clear, clean windows of childhood, the memories preserved for a lifetime.

Each Pullman car had its own evocative name. By the time we got back to our sleeping car, passing through "Savannah River," "Island Home," "Rice Bird" and others, our porter would be making up the berths. Reaching way up, his white jacket hiked high over tight shiny black trousers, standing on tiptoe in his polished black boots, he let down the khaki-colored upper berth, using a special lug wrench that he had unsnapped from its place by the small rotating fan near the ceiling. All the blankets and sheets, and the red and green striped mattress for the lower berth were stored up there.

He shrugged the pillows into their cases with a snap; hooked up the little ladder, and then buttoned on the green webbing that was supposed to keep the occupant of the top bunk from falling out. This turned out to be just the thing for playing Tarzan. In the upper berth, I'd stick my arms and legs through the gaps, while he made up the lower, joking and storytelling all the while, ducking his head good-naturedly to avoid my swinging feet.

First the snowy bottom sheet was tucked snugly over the mattress, then came a top sheet, two tan and yellow patterned blankets, with PULLMAN CO. woven into the wool, and a third sheet over that for a blanket cover. A spare blanket was rolled into a tight cylinder under the window, the pillows plumped up, and finally the bed was turned down in an inviting fold. All this took about ten minutes. Then the porter wrote down our destination for the morning wake-up call, and reminded us to leave our shoes in the little two-way hinged compartment if we wanted them polished during the night.

In the bathroom there was fresh ice water in the thermos jug in its bracket near the round, gleaming stainless steel sink, and a holder filled with elegant paper-cone cups. A sign over the toilet contained a memorable warning, and all us children sang its words to the melody of Dvorak's *Humoresque*:

**Passengers Will Please Refrain**
**From Flushing Toilet When The Train**
**Is Standing In The Station**

When you flushed, you got a strong whiff of cinders, a blast of cold air on your bottom, and—through the open flap in the bowl—a mysterious glimpse of the gravelly railroad bed noisily zipping by underneath.

Better not to wonder what happened to what you did. The grownups would never discuss it anyway. They were odd about toilets. My mother always admonished me to use one of the slippery tissue paper seat covers she brought with her on trips, or else she would arrange little segments of toilet paper around the seat, but they always slipped off before I could sit down, and I couldn't see the point of them anyway.

Later, in my lower berth, swaying in the clickity-clacking dark after Marg went to sleep in the upper, I would pinch the brass catch and slide up the dark green shade. Propped up on the high pillows, I watched the land rocketing by under the starlight.

I always tried to stay awake at least until Washington, where I could see the wondrous sight of the great floodlit Capitol Dome, and the luminous obelisk of the Washington Monument floating in the black sky, like the magic Emerald City of Oz. After that, sleep would overcome me until we were jolted awake at Richmond. There the train switched tracks and joined the Atlantic Coastline system; jerking, hissing and clanging as it whizzed and creaked backwards, the apparently random maneuvers ending with a crash as it coupled on a new dining car or changed engines.

Robert Benchley once wrote that whenever he took the sleeper train south he was sure the engineer allowed his eight-year-old nephew to practice driving the engine in the middle of the night, and that's exactly how it felt!

I would hurriedly yank down the shade when the train pulled into the station, for fear someone would look in the window and see me in bed in my pajamas. Lying on my stomach, squinting through the crack at the very bottom of the blind, I'd spy on the brawny workers towing long heavy carts piled high with gray mail sacks and passengers hurrying for the train. Far down the track you could see the brakeman signaling with a lantern.

These were the days of the Depression, and it is hard for me to believe now that I was not aware of class or poverty or that people might resent a small, rich person lying there in the Pullman sleeper when so many other children were sitting up uncomfortably all night long in the coaches.

At first light, I'd raise the shade again and with a thrill gaze out over a totally changed landscape: the South, so completely different from home. The train was now jiggling comfortably over flat sandy soil, past tall, narrow tobacco-drying sheds and acres of longleaf and loblolly pine. In just one night we had left behind factories and cities and rolling pastures and winter-bare woodlands. The colors were shades of washed-out beige, contrasting with the soft green of the pines. The stubble in the cornfields was pale gold, and the morning light flooded over fallow fields of tawny broom sedge. Gray cypress trees with hanks of Spanish moss caught limply in their spindly branches stood in swamp water that gleamed black as ink.

The land was unfenced and the crossings were without signals except for the warning whistle of the train. The engine often killed cattle that grazed between the rails, and trucks and jalopies frequently stalled on the tracks. It was a rare trip when something wasn't hit. When the train stopped, we'd all get out and stare at the accident.

Because of these hazards our progress slowed once we reached the Carolinas. There was time to absorb the intimate details of the dearly familiar Southern landscape, as we steamed close by unpainted or whitewashed cabins that were set up off the ground on shaky brick columns.

Dark pine smoke spiraled from their leaning chimneys and drifted into the blue Carolina sky. Typically, a black three-legged iron pot for washing clothes sat out front in the yard, and the path to the cabin was lined with whitewashed automobile tires balanced on their ends. A few scrawny chickens and a big old rooster might be pecking in the dust, and a rickety pigpen leaned precariously against a gum tree. Inside their pen, the lean black hogs were waiting for breakfast, their wet pink noses snuffling against the boards.

I saw two women sitting out on the front steps of their cabin already smoking clay pipes. Their little girls, hair braided into spiky pigtails, skipped about waving at the passing train. A boy in faded denim bib overalls hung around solemn and shy, and skinny hound dogs gazed out mournfully from under the porch.

Out in the field a farmer leaned on the handles of his plow, turning over the earth for an early crop of collards or tobacco, his mule plodding steadily onward, ears wagging, head down. Another day was beginning.

The train crept right through the center of the towns, which all seemed alike, with wide empty streets fronted by one- and two-story buildings. There were loan offices, pawnbrokers, department stores, 5&10's, the corner bank, the feed and grain store, the ornate movie theater, many churches, and usually a courthouse with an imposing pillared portico.

This was a land where the white sheriff's word was the Law, the Baptist and African Methodist Episcopal churches furnished hope and comfort, and there were separate public toilets for Men, Women, and Colored.

Kingstree, our destination, was a flag stop on the Atlantic Coastline Railroad. It was named for the immensely tall longleaf pines preferred by the British for the masts of the Royal Navy in the eighteenth century. The same pines are to be found in the forests today, now even more valuable because of their scarcity.

We had arrived! Our sixteen bags, the gun cases and the frantic dogs—bursting with excitement and other things—were safely set out on the wooden platform that stretched between long tobacco sheds and storehouses filled with overstuffed bales of cotton. The most surprising thing was to feel the balmy air on my skin after the dank chill we had left behind in the North.

Our porter was tipped about two dollars per family for all his uncomplaining work, and he bowed and ducked his head smiling extravagant thanks—astonished and grateful, or so he wanted us to believe. After picking up the little yellow stool he had set out as an aid in dismounting, he waved goodbye to us with his cap, leaning way out from the Pullman car, his white jacket reflecting the sunlight as the train dwindled away, clacking on down to Georgia.

The men from our plantation were always there to meet us. I can still hear their soft Gullah accents, their jokes and their affectionate happy greetings. I loved them all, and their welcomes live on in my heart.

# 14

## *Friendfield Plantation*

After the overnight train ride from Philadelphia, the fifty-mile drive from the railroad station at Kingstree to the plantation on the flat, two-lane highway, bordered by featureless pine forest and small pastures, seemed to take an eternity. The ride was enlivened, however, by the comical stories told by Pat McClary, longtime manager of our family's plantation, and every child's best friend.

Pat had a thick Southern accent, spoke the local Gullah dialect, and possessed a never-ending repertoire of jokes and funny tales. He was a large man, big of girth and big of heart, who lived for hunting and shooting, for family and country, and for the care of Friendfield Plantation. He would remain the resident manager there for forty-two years, from 1930 to 1972. He was a grandfather figure for me, and later for my own children. Bouncing around in the back of his pickup truck, as he sped along the rutted dirt roads of the plantation spotting game—possums, coons, deer, owls, hawks, or (heaven forbid) stray cats—was my idea of happiness.

The truck would lurch to a halt, crack went the .22 rifle, and—before our horrified eyes—that was the end of the cat. (They ate the quail eggs and couldn't be tolerated; just another predator.) This sounds cruel, but shotguns and rifles and hunting were an everyday part of my world in those days, and we were trained under rigorous safety rules.

Once, driving home from the station, Pat told me a disturbing story. I was just a little girl and never questioned the local customs; I accepted the system as "just the way things were" in the South. He told about the time a cow crossed over from her unfenced pasture onto Highway 526 and was killed by our pickup. It could have caused a nasty accident, but there was little damage to truck or passengers. Pat told James the driver to load the cow into the truck, take her back to the kennel, cut her up and "feed her to de dawgs."

Because of the lack of fencing along the highway, farmers had no rights. Loose stock wandered at their own risk, and road kill was fair game. I felt sad for the farmer, and sorry for the cow, and a first glimmering of rural Southern attitudes in those days began to dawn on me. The farmer was never even notified, much less compensated.

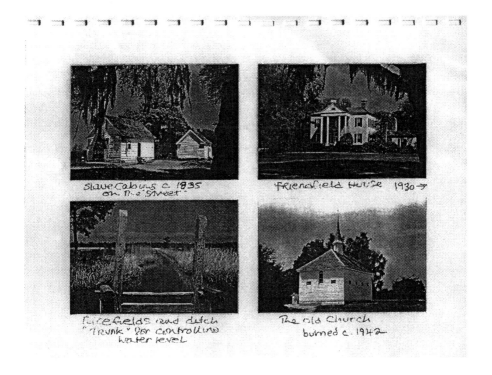

slave cabins c. 1835 on the "street"

Friendfield House 1930→

ricefields and ditch "Trunk" for controlling water level

The old Church burned c. 1942

Friendfield Plantation was bought by my father in 1930, and it has belonged to our family ever since. It is rare nowadays in America for a family property to pass down through the generations, and it is especially poignant to watch children and grandchildren responding to the timeless beauty and charm of this old rice plantation, just as I did seventy-five years ago.

My grandchildren are proud of the big old house, and look forward to the delicious Southern cooking and baking: cornbread, hot biscuits (with butter balls and honey), venison, quail, wild turkey, cooter soup (made from the local yellow-bellied marsh turtle), crabmeat, shrimp, pecan pie, and prune soufflé. My grandchildren respect the old traditions, and even enjoy dressing for dinner in the formal dining room. The beautifully set mahogany table under its crystal chandelier, the candlelight, the centerpiece of camellias, and the hot, sparking pinewood fire giving off its resiny smell create an evocative and ongoing memory.

When a youngster is finally allowed to join in the quail hunt, it is a thrilling day. The young first-time hunter rides out on his pony with the rest of the shooting party, following the well-trained bird dogs (pointers or setters) while they search out elusive coveys. The dogs hunt eagerly, ranging far, but obeying the shrill whistle of their trainer. Brambles often rip their lolling tongues as they plunge heedlessly in and out of ditches and swamp-edge at full run.

Then a pointer freezes, tail stiff, head and nose turned toward the invisible bird. The dog handler yells, *"Point!"* The teenager leaps off his pony, pulls the shotgun from its scabbard, carefully slips the shells in the chamber, makes sure the safety is on, and, trembling with trepidation, walks stealthily up to the pointer, who is inhaling the heady smell of *quail* so intensely that its whole body quivers with suppressed longing. The suspense is heightened if the dogs are not exactly up with the birds, and the hunter follows them, his heart thumping, jumping at each little sound, while they creep along stealthily, trailing the birds through the feed patch of lespedeza brush. "Careful, careful, hunt close, hunt close," cautions the handler to his dogs, at the same time motioning the young hunter not to hang back.

Suddenly, always unexpectedly, the covey erupts with a huge whirr of wings, *whizz*, the little birds fly every which way, and our terrified boy, in desperation, fires into the middle of the flight, forgetting the admonition to pick out one bird and sight on it. Miracle of miracles, a bird falls. "Hunt daid, hunt daid," encourages the handler, and after a long tail-wagging search one of the dogs picks up the dead bird and presents it to the triumphant shooter. This is one of the proudest days a youngster could have. The first quail! A landmark day for a neophyte hunter, and one he will never forget.

The exciting paddle in the mysterious before-dawn dark into the marsh in a flat-bottomed wooden punt was another memorable experience. Invisible coots chuckled and rustled in the reeds, and occasionally a startled mallard flushed, rising up in the dark with a beating of wings and harsh, noisy quacking. The anxious wait in the blind for the first rushing flight of ducks that appear from nowhere brings the same excitement today as in my own now distant youth, and the ducks are still just as hard to hit.

Some mornings were so cold that the boatmen, Wesley and James, had to crack the ice with their paddles before they could make it out to the corn shuck blinds in the middle of the pond. The colder and more blustery the weather, the more stirred up the ducks became. The ringnecks and teal would go ripping overhead, my shot following far behind. I almost never hit one because I couldn't seem to lead them sufficiently, or spot them coming over the decoys in time to aim. I'd have to sit there freezing until Daddy got his limit, and I thought I would perish each time. After all, he could lean out of the blind to relieve himself, and I was trapped inside my canvas britches and layers of long underwear.

In other parts of the country, hunters use retrievers to swim out and bring back the wounded or dead ducks, but at our place the danger from gators and water moccasins made swimming in the ponds too risky for the Labradors and spaniels. In the past, many gators were shot, and when cut open, revealed grisly dog collar mementos.

At the end of the hunt, the boatman picked up the ducks. I always felt sorry for the waiting men, who had to crouch for hours on the edge of the rice field during those freezing mornings, marking where each duck went down.

One memorable morning an otter surged up and took a wounded struggling duck off the water right in front of the blind, depriving Daddy of the evidence he needed to prove he had gotten his limit. But then, armed with that unusual excuse, home we went to a big breakfast of grits and pancakes in the cozy dining room, in front of a roaring fire.

Friendfield eventually grew to include about 3,000 acres, as my father gradually pieced together numerous small farm holdings that brought the property back to its former antebellum acreage. The land, bordered by White's Creek, Port's Creek and the Sampit River, is a typical low country mixture of rice fields, marsh and upland forests of loblolly and longleaf pine.

The original property, circa 1730, belonged to James Withers, a wealthy Charleston brickmaker, indigo planter, and rice planter. His son, Francis, built the big Friendfield house in 1818. A newspaper clipping of the day records that it was "a large mansion of English brick noted over the whole countryside." The article describes front steps and porch of flagstone, decorative wrought-iron railings and elaborate 19th century scenic wallpaper from France ("Monuments of Paris" by Dufour) in the parlor. A grand circular staircase extended from the ground floor to the attic. There were doorknobs of silver, fine oil paintings and an excellent library. Apparently all the notables, including the governor of South Carolina and the mayor of Georgetown, attended the housewarming.

In the years before the War Between the States (the Civil War was always called that by Southerners), the rice planters in the Carolina low country were immensely wealthy and cultured. They often traveled abroad, and sent their sons to universities like Harvard. In the 18th century, the little seaport town of Georgetown, five miles from Friendfield, shipped out more tons of rice—"Carolina Gold," the long grain seed from Madagascar—than any other port in the world, even sending rice to China.

After the Civil War, the house passed through many hands, and gradually fell into disrepair. In 1922, Patrick Cleburn McClary of Georgetown bought the house and leased it to a duck-hunting club. It burned to the ground in 1926. My father sternly informed us that this was because the men got drunk and didn't tend to the log fire. It was a scary lesson for us in a house where every room has an open fireplace.

My father purchased the land and ruined mansion in 1930, and rebuilt it using the original floor plan. When he started the project, the property surrounding the "big house" was overgrown with thick brush, and visitors had to push their way up through the tangles of vines and brambles from the landing at White's Creek to the original house site. Only the avenue of ancient live oaks, the chimneys and part of the foundations remained standing. My father's guide was Pat McClary, son of the last owner, who soon became our first manager. Daddy called Pat from his home in Philadelphia to suggest that he start off his job on a trial basis, "because you might not suit me after we get going." Pat, a proud Southerner, replied, "I agree to that, Mr. Cheston, because you are a Yankee and you might not suit *me.*" The "trial," not without some hot arguments, lasted 42 years.

By about 1900, rice was no longer grown commercially in the area. The crop had created enormous wealth for the Carolina planters in the days when they counted on intensive slave labor to plant and harvest. After the turn of the century, because of two devastating hurricanes in a row and the end of cheap labor, rice was not a commercially viable crop. The sticky black mud called "pluff" bogged down oxen, mules and tractors, and only manpower could work those once valuable rice fields. Today, most of the former rice fields have reverted to tidal marsh and federal law prohibits man-made construction in wetlands. Even hundred-year-old dikes and ditches cannot be repaired legally.

A few years ago, an elderly, irascible plantation-owner friend of ours got so mad at a federal officer who ordered him to stop fixing a breach in one of his dikes that he chased him off with a shotgun. I don't know what the outcome was. Southerners still passionately resent government interference of any kind.

Some rice for home consumption was raised on Friendfield until 1942. I remember, when I was a child, watching the plantation women using traditional techniques, flailing and winnowing the rice, near the old sagging rice barn. Both the barn and the rice mill have since been torn down for safety's sake.

Timber, the chief source of plantation revenue then and now, was carefully controlled, and areas were selectively cut each summer. The entire upland property was burned over each spring, to keep down the undergrowth and litter, fire lines were ploughed, and the land managed for quail and wildlife propagation. If the litter and brush were left unchecked, hunting dogs and shooting ponies couldn't travel through the woods, and the lespedeza and millet patches to attract the wild quail could not be planted. Longleaf pine is fire resistant so the burning process did not damage this valuable crop.

My family's life on the plantation was centered on hunting quail and ducks, and deer and turkey in their seasons. They spent much of the winter after Christmas, as well as part of March and April, in South Carolina, and I joined them whenever I had school vacations.

The plantation workers and tenant farmers lived in small, whitewashed cabins, scattered throughout the property. The cabins were set up off the ground on brick pillars, away from the rising damp and visiting snakes. Until the 1940's, these workers lived without electricity or indoor plumbing.

We knew all of the families, cared about them, and visited with them often. They raised many children, tended small gardens, and kept a few pigs and chickens and a plowing mule. We thought they were happy and raggedly carefree, and they greeted us with unfailing courtesy and smiles. The old slave quarters, where many of those families lived, still exist on each side of "the Street," a white sand road leading out back of the "Big House" to the barnyard.

Threshing Rice At Friendfield   c 1935

I used to go there almost every day to play marbles and skip rope with the children. I didn't go inside the cabins for some reason, perhaps it wasn't allowed, but I remember peeking into the dark rooms whose walls were papered over with newspapers for insulation. Typically, there were three rooms: two small bedrooms and one bigger room for eating, sitting, and cooking over an open hearth. The light was from kerosene lanterns, but everyone turned in as soon as it grew dark, just as they do in a village in Africa.

There was an outhouse, about twenty yards in back, and an outdoor hand pump at the well. I loved to prime the pump with water from the tin cup always left full nearby. The handle made a tremendous squeaking and clanking noise, and then came the squelch of suction and the satisfying gush of water. The washing was done in the yard, in a big cast-iron, three-legged pot, the water heated by a hot pinewood fire. Hogs snorted and rooted in makeshift pens in the thick swampy woods behind the cabins.

Small gardens were planted with early collard greens in the winter months. In the spring and summer larger communal gardens grew yams and watermelons, peas and beans. The men were keen hunters of deer, possum, squirrel, raccoon and rabbit, and there were always catfish, flounder, bream, turtles, blue crabs and shrimp to be caught or trapped in the rice field ponds and ditches. I'm sure more than a few ducks were bagged when the boss was up north.

Pat told me a story about a man over on George Vanderbilt's Arcadia Plantation who shot his wife's lover dead. He was convicted of murder and sentenced to the chain gang for life. At the same time another man from Arcadia was convicted of poaching wood ducks, and he was sentenced to six months in jail.

But the murderer happened to be Mr. Vanderbilt's cook, a good one, and Mr. Vanderbilt wanted him back. So Mr. V. had a few words with the sheriff, and the murderer was sprung after a week.

The poacher complained from his cell: "What kind of a state we live in, when de law turn a man loose for murder, and I serve six months in de jail house fo' getting' me a few ducks?"

The cabin dwellers showed us only deferential kindness and humor; their inner lives and thoughts were hidden from us whites. It was years before I understood the survival mechanisms of Southern "coloreds," which was always to agree and give the answer that white folks expect, and come up with an ingenious ready excuse.

"Yassuh Boss, I done wash de dishes keerful lak you always done 'splain me, but dat plate seem lak it tuk wings an fly from me han' by he ownself lak a quail." Just about everyone who worked for us in those days spoke Gullah, the local coastal Carolina patois that is a combination of their tribal African language and English.

In the house, Maggie and Liza were the chambermaid and waitress. In duck hunting season, besides their daily duties, they were expected to rise at five and light the pinewood fires in the icy bedrooms for those hunters going out early to the blinds.

Drayton, the butler, took justifiable pride in his duties, and ruled over Miss Florence, the cook, and the rest of the household with total authority. The women in the house always deferred to the men, at least *almost* always. Drayton carved the meat, filleted the shad, cut up the venison, passed the drinks and waited on table.

I watched when Drayton butchered a cooter or a snapping turtle for the dinner table. He looped a rope around a sturdy stick, then teased the turtle until it made a lightning fast snapping bite to grab and hold on with its sharp, beak-like jaws. He ordered me to pull the stick away slowly so that the poor turtle extended its neck, and then he chopped off its head with one quick blow of the axe. I watched, appalled, while the turtle crawled about, headless and bleeding. The warning went that if a snapper ever latched on to you, he wouldn't let go until there was a thunderstorm. Afterwards, I was supposed to enjoy the soup, even when I spotted the turtle's tail and paws with claws and all, floating about in the broth with the carrots and meat.

My father tried, without success, to make me eat live oyster crabs: tiny crisp critters that ran about on top of a raw oyster served on the half shell. I tried it once. When I reluctantly attempted to swallow the oyster, the little crab scurried across my tongue until I could catch it between my teeth with a crunch! Never again, though fried oyster crabs and whitebait were a prime delicacy for the grownups.

Drayton always ate his meals standing up, leaning on the pantry counter. He told me: "I bin a steward in the United States Navy, and I got a habit of eatin' dat way." (As the only man on the indoor staff, I think he wanted to avoid eating in the kitchen with the household of women.) He was an upstanding, dignified man, and the money he saved from his job helped educate his son, who became principal of the local school and the first black resident of Georgetown to earn a Masters degree. We were all very proud of him.

Later on, Liza's only daughter got her Ph.D. in education and became principal of a special education school in Harlem. She traveled to conferences all over Europe. When Liza retired, her daughter bought her a tidy brick house on Queen Street in Georgetown, where we often visited her. Liza was a wise and exceptional lady.

At that time, older women, both black and white, were always called by the title "Miss" before their first name. I am still "Miss Frances" at the age of 80, and our cook is "Miss Pauline." The older white men were always called "Cap'n" or "Mister."

In those days the house servants wore ankle-length, full-skirted, madras plaid dresses with matching turbans and starched white aprons. Today that domestic uniform would be unacceptable as Aunt Jemima stereotyping. They were the kindest, most loving people, and their special blend of sympathetic friendship and religious faith remains a comforting and inspiring memory.

The cabins for the outdoor workers were on the street in back of the Big House. There were no porches, and the women and old folks sat on their front steps, smoking their white clay pipes, resting and sunning and gossiping, watching the "chilluns" at play. I loved talking to old Rev. and I remember visiting with him when he was sitting on his step, holding his grandbaby. An ancient Gullah woman called Ma'am Pleasant, who was noted for her *unpleasant* disposition, complained to me: "Lookit at dat wuthless ol' man. He love he grand too much, so he cain't stan' fer a fly to light on her. Too bad he ain't pay de same attention to us'uns needin' de wood split and chores handle."

When her husband, Jim, a lovely gentle soul, was dying, Ma'am Pleasant was heard to say, "Why that old fool take so long to die anyway? I wish de Lawd would come down and tak him up right now so we don't haf to bin waitin' around dis away."

Another time Rev. told me: "Whooee, las' winter was so cold dat me an' my wife was dreamin' de same dreams!" I picture him walking along at the edge of the swamp, in his faded denim bib overalls, trying to herd a scraggly line of black and white spotted piglets that were racing to the corn trough. He kept on chastising them with a long stick, as though they were disobedient children: "Hey, pig what you doin'? Stop that foolin'. Git along this way or I'm gonna whup yo' rear end! Yo' sho' goin' make me a fine barbeque, if yo' don't mind me!"

The cabin windows had no screens. At nightfall the shutters were closed to keep out the ha'nts (ghosts), especially the dreaded *plat eye*. The plat eye possessed a supernatural ability to imitate the familiar voice of a family member. At nighttime, it was said to lure many a person out of bed, enticing the victim to a watery death in the swamp. There really were some incidents of drowning in the swamp...but the "plat eye" that killed these victims was actually hallucination and delusion brought about by the high fever of malaria or yellow fever, the scourges of earlier plantation living.

Wesley Bright and his wife Maybell and their kids were another of my favorite families. Their eldest daughter was the beautiful and errant Ruth, who kept running away with different men. Another daughter, Jessie May, the boys Curtis and Wesley Jr. and the triplets Alvin, Alton, and Annette, were packed together in their small cabin at the barnyard. The Bright household wasn't the most crowded. Tom Joiner, the dog man and huntsman, and his jolly fat wife Dolly had ten "head" of children under their roof; it seemed as if each year there was another adorable baby. Tom allowed as how he wasn't exactly sure how many there were, and when my own daughter Frances was about seven or eight, Dolly told her that she "plumb done run out of names." She asked Frances to suggest a name for their youngest baby. Frances said, without hesitation, "Call her Pollyanna." "Lawd hab mussy, dat's a sweet name," Dolly beamed, and so she was christened.

That name turned out to be lucky. About thirty years later, Pollyanna drove up to the Big House in a fancy black sedan, wearing a beautiful mink coat. She was showing her husband the plantation and the rickety little cabin where she had been brought up. I was delighted to meet her again, and to learn that she held an advanced surgical nursing degree from Stanford University. She and her husband lived in San Francisco where he was a successful medical malpractice lawyer.

Many children were brought up in those tiny cabins. The school bus showed up every day for those whose parents bothered to send them. Some made it, like Pollyanna, but many didn't. Were they really happy? Did they complain? I never knew, but I did learn that Wesley drank too much.

Pat told me that when he bailed Wesley out of jail for the umpteenth time, he told him: "Wesley! Good Lawd, man, why you keep on doin' that way when y'all know how much aggravation it causes?"

Wesley grinned his delightful grin, and answered, "Cap'n Pat, you just ain't never been a nigger on Saturday night." In those days, the Negroes referred to themselves with the "N" word, and it was often part of colloquial dialogue on such popular radio programs as *Amos and Andy*. Wesley lived to a ripe old age, in spite of his carousing. I went to his funeral, and he looked handsome and young in his open casket when I went up to the altar to say goodbye to him, and thank him for all our good times together when I was a child.

Francis Withers built a wooden church, in an unusual Gothic style, on the street as a meetinghouse for his slaves. In his will, dated 1848, he stipulated that the services should have a preacher for "as long as the people desired it." Although a slave owner like all his white South Carolina plantation-owning neighbors, he was extremely kind and thoughtful and left numerous bequests of $5000 and more to his widespread family and friends. He left his wife "the Friendfield gang of 200 slaves," with the stipulation that the families never be separated, and made arrangements for an old slave retainer to be housed comfortably with a relative of his in Georgetown for the remainder of her life.

There is a burying ground for the house slaves near the Big House, and although most of the wooden grave markers have rotted away, the many depressions in the earth tell of multiple burials. One special one that remains is a simple brick and carved stone, which reads simply, "Jane." She was a favorite nurse for the children and grandchildren of the Withers family. No last name was recorded.

Another burying ground is a mile beyond the Street, and families whose people were born at Friendfield still come from faraway cities like Buffalo, New York, to bury their dead near their ancestors. Until recently, personal items like spectacles and shaving mugs were left on the graves for the use of their owners in the Promised Land.

I loved to go to that little whitewashed church to listen to the singing, clapping and "praise Jesus-ing!" that went along with the fervent praying. Once when I was about ten, they asked me to read a Bible verse from the pulpit, which I did, proudly. At that time many of the adults were illiterate, and it was unusual for a young'un to be able to read. The little group of people clapped for me, and chorused "A-men," the usual response of affirmation.

These traditional Gullah services were called "Sing, Shout and Praise" meetings. The accompaniment to the songs (not called hymns) was a complex, rhythmic contrapuntal hand-clapping and foot-stomping. The shouting was a testimonial to Jesus. There was sometimes a tambourine, rarely a piano, and the religious fervor often caused one or two in the female congregation to be seized by the spirit. These ladies would swoon, and they had to be supported and fanned by some of the sisters.

The sermons delivered at top volume by the all-powerful preacher were hell-fire and damnation, and you had to be pretty confident that you weren't a sinner to hold up your head when on the receiving end. The sisters sat on one side of the aisle, the important deacons on the other, and the rest of the congregation behind. The children dressed in their Sunday best, and the women wore decorated hats.

You had to walk up to the pulpit with your offering. The money was totaled up then and there, under the watchful eyes of the deacons, and the amount announced: "fo' dollars and twenty-one cents." The first two counts were never deemed sufficient, and everyone had to divvy up again.

I love and appreciate the South Carolina A.M.E. and Baptist Church services, especially the heartfelt singing. We often attended the New Providence Baptist Church near Pawleys's Island. Peter Small, the butler who succeeded Drayton, was the senior deacon, and he arranged for special "programs" to be incorporated into the service. There were solo and choir Gospel singers, and music that had us jumping in the aisles. Later, my kids always said, "If our church was like that, we'd go every Sunday!"

The sincere belief in Jesus and the promise of the hereafter gave the Negroes hope and solace when life was hard and there was little to be thankful for. Whites like my children and myself have always been welcomed into their churches, with great courtesy and warmth. The funerals are moving testimonials of faith. They are called "home going" services: a lovely idea for welcoming the deceased.

I had no understanding then about the harsh rules of segregation, except when I wasn't allowed to have one of my "colored" friends (we didn't say "Black" or "African American" in those days) from the Street to the Big House for a meal. I could invite a girl friend in to play jacks, but when it was time for lunch, she would slip away to the kitchen, where I would join her after eating in the dining room. We both accepted that as normal.

One time, and much more puzzling, was when I wasn't allowed to bring a colored playmate with me to the beach at Pawley's Island. I learned later that colored people were actually banned from that beach in the mid-1930's. I made a big fuss, because this interfered with my plans to have a friend to play with on the beach, to no avail. Why? It didn't make sense to me, but again, my friend accepted the decision without argument and we drove off without her.

Once a guest made a disparaging remark about the house servants—a dreadful racist slur. She said loudly, at the dinner table, "I wonder if we smell as bad to them as they do to us." I blushed furiously, and ducked my head to hide hot, quick tears, so afraid that Drayton or Liza might have overheard and had their feelings hurt. These and other incidents started me off on a lifelong resentment of racism, and snobbery.

Friendfield House was restored under the direction of architect Arthur Meigs, of the Philadelphia firm of Mellor and Meigs. Pillars two stories tall support the front porch in classical fashion, and a graceful Italianate arcade leads up from the sandy driveway in the back.

The rooms were big and square, with thirteen-foot ceilings and tall windows. A charming floral needlepoint rug brightened the parlor, the furniture there was antique, and an ornate gilt pier mirror reached from floor to ceiling. The curtains were red velvet, suitable for one of Miss Scarlett's makeover wartime gowns.

My great, great grandfather, Francis Martin Drexel's lovely portrait of a serious little girl, hangs over the mantel. She is also wearing a floor length red velvet dress, a white ruffled cap over her curls, and forever pulls her little toy wooden wagon over the oriental carpet. A fine portrait of Alexander Hamilton, attributed to Robert Fulton, is on the far wall.

The children were not allowed to play in the parlor, although we always managed to sneak in and raid the enticing purple tin of Camee chocolates at their accustomed place on the round mahogany table. If a grownup should be tempted to look inside, they would find the bottom layer consisted of cleverly concealed spit-backs, those icky ones with runny liqueur centers. We thought the room immensely grand, and we tried to behave ourselves when we were invited in.

The library was a cozy room, paneled in cypress, with one semi-circular wall whose shelves were filled with well-thumbed novels old and new, wildlife reference books, mysteries, and non-fiction tales of adventure. A unique collection of oil paintings of World War I allies in their regimental uniforms hung on the opposite wall and over the fireplace. The room was hospitably shabby, a place where the hunters could plop down in their old clothes to enjoy drinks or tea by the fire, and dogs were always welcome.

Umberto Innocenti, a famous landscape architect from Florence, Italy directed the restoration of the original gardens, and designed the decorative brick walls enclosing the camellia garden, the paths and fountains. Red, white and pink camellias still bloom profusely during the winter months, making each glossy green-leafed bush resemble a decorated Christmas tree. In March, all the glories of spring emerge: azaleas, daffodils, wisteria, jasmine and gardenias. Later, in May, the powerful sensuous perfume from the huge waxy-white blooms of magnolia grandiflora drifts in the soft spring air.

On its south side, the house faces out over sweeping lawns toward rice fields and river. The lawn, planted each fall in rye grass, is always a startling bright green, even in winter. The giant live oaks in the "big yard" are more than two hundred years old, draped with graceful curly fronds of gray Spanish moss that trail to the ground from their thick, spreading branches. Horned owls nest there in precarious nests, and in mating season (late January) the sound of their mournful *whoo-whooing* echoes through the dusky night.

Our houseman, rascally Fraser, had formerly worked at the neighboring plantation Hobcaw Barony, owned by Bernard Baruch. Fraser told me that Cap'n Baruch kept pet horned owls that walked up and down the steps like little old men. I would have loved to see that!

The little owlets, looking like balls of gray fluff, often fell from their nests, and restoring them to their homes meant having to climb up onto the last rung of the tallest extension ladder to reach the nest. Once, while on such a mission, our present manager, Virgil Dugan was struck on the back of his neck by one of the adult owls. He was knocked off the ladder, and the claw wounds required six stitches.

Another time, an adult owl became annoyed at me when I ventured too close to the tree where the owlets were staring down at me. I heard a loud clacking noise and saw the big mother owl advancing across the field toward me on clawed feet, feathers puffed out to create the look of a giant gargoyle, snapping her beak and glaring with malevolent yellow eyes. I didn't wait around to see what she might do next.

When I was a teenager, I tried to keep a baby owl as a pet. I was a poor mouser and only managed to trap about three of the mice in our corncrib. These I dangled by their tails over the owlet's head as I imagined a parent owl might do. Snap! Gulp! The mice vanished, with only a little bit of one mouse's tail dangling from the owlet's beak. I couldn't catch any more mice, so the next day I contrived to mold raw hamburger on the end of a string. After the gulp, the string was pulled out, and my invention solved the feeding problem! My pet owl survived well until his wings fledged out, and then we turned him loose.

The poetic sweetness of the Carolina low country landscape and the sounds of my childhood there still resonate today: the birdsong, the nightly shrilling of tree frogs, the chuckling, quacking voices of coots and ducks, the croaks of the heron, and the booming of bullfrogs in the marsh. Sometimes I am awakened by the distant barking of the bird dogs and hounds in their kennels, as they alert us to the passing of a predator. Gators still patrol the rice fields, and in the spring they bellow and roar as they search for a mate. One night I caught a gator in the beam of my flashlight when I walked along the rice field bank in the dark, and his eyes gleamed red as coals, as he cruised silently and sinisterly in the ditch canal. They have a mirror-like membrane behind the eyeball that enhances their night vision.

One year, the soft April night was made even more mysterious by the mournful screams of our resident peacock, George, lonesome for his mate, who had been eaten as she sat on their eggs.

The serpentine water gardens behind the big house had been dug out of a cypress swamp in the early 1800's by prodigious slave labor. With Pat's help, the original outlines of this "sunken garden" were discovered and then restored under the direction of Mr. Innocenti, when he went about marking special specimen trees and shrubs. He was delighted when Pat pointed out that the first tea plants ever to be planted in South Carolina were still growing near the house.

In March and April, the black tannic water reflects azaleas, confederate jasmine, wisteria, and cascading Cherokee roses. The graceful blue heron spears fish there, cronking as he flaps away. He and the snowy egret are the loveliest birds with the ugliest voices. A prehistoric-looking anhinga roosts on a low branch drying his black outstretched wings. He looks at me with his beady eye and takes to the water, like a pterodactyl reincarnated. His long slender neck and rapier-like bill gave him the well-chosen name of "snake bird." Egrets are locally called "Po Joe's" (no good to eat).

The water garden was a magical place for me when I was a child, and my children and grandchildren paddle the same kind of flat-bottomed boat around the islands, as I did, pretending to be Indian warriors, or pirate captains.

I have never revealed the place where I buried my treasure seventy years ago, or confessed that the brassbound chest of legend was really a cardboard box containing some pennies, nickels and cookies. However, the crumpled map with its "bloodstains" (ketchup) and X marking the spot still exists, saved by my mother and father in the desk drawer. My friend Shirley and I signed it, in what we thought of as pirate script: "One-eyed Pete, Captain and Stinking Bill, Mate."

On the plantation there was always something interesting and exciting to do, and we made up our own fun. There was a derelict house, Silver Hill, originally called Mount Pleasant, up in the barnyard; a big square three-story building made of weathered, unpainted cypress, supported by tall brick pillars. It was almost totally dark inside because the windows were boarded up with plywood, and the wide pine boards were loose and dangerous on the upper floors. My playmates and I bet the family that we would be brave enough to spend the night inside, among the huge field rats and the bats and spiders. Naturally they could offer us large rewards with impunity, for the grownups knew that we would be far too chicken-hearted to last more than about half an hour.

The old abandoned house was later identified as a 1791 mansion with lovely proportioned rooms, fourteen-foot ceilings, carved cornices and fireplaces. Plantation slaves, who were skilled carpenters and bricklayers, built the house for Robert Withers, a son of the first owner of Friendfield. It remained unoccupied and derelict after his death in 1830. Silver Hill is the only existing example of a plantation house built in the "vernacular" in our region of the low country that had not been modified in any way since the 18th century—no additions, plumbing, or electricity. It was a forgotten building and wasn't listed on the tax rolls, a fact my father did not hasten to correct. The old house survived many hurricanes, including Hugo, which was strong enough to blow a steel tugboat over the rice fields onto the front lawn. Not even a brick fell out of the chimneys.

1791 Silver Hill Plantation House at Friendfield

A plantation Christmas party for the children of the workers used to be held at Silver Hill every year, and "Sandy Claw" doled out the gifts that had been individually wrapped by our manager's wife, Jessie, who called each child by name to come forward to receive the oranges and toys. She told me she had to wrap at least a dozen extra for all the friends and relations who had a way of showing up for the party. The rest of the time the old mansion house stayed empty, used only to store hay and scrap lumber. It has now been meticulously restored to its former splendor by my ex son-in-law, Daniel Thorne, but back then we only thought of it as our old wreck of a haunted house.

Friendfield was where I saw my father most. Being the youngest child, I could skip a few weeks of school on each end of regular vacations.

He helped me (impatiently) with my hated math workbooks and took me on long tramps through the rice fields on the muddy dikes. He identified the birds and ducks for me, and we were both keenly interested in the moccasins, gators, fiddler crabs and bullfrogs. We were good companions in those days.

Everyone respected my father but we were all scared of him. When he walked in the rice fields, loyal Drayton had to follow him out to the marsh—still wearing his butler's white coat and black trousers—with a silver tray bearing the glass of milk that my father was supposed to drink every two hours. That was the diet for ulcers then: creamed food and rich milk, a prescription that eventually contributed to his heart disease and strokes.

Out hunting, my father always wore a twill jacket, tweed woolen necktie, neat woolen shirt, and greased knee-high Gokey snake-proof boots. James Graham, the dog handler, always maintained that "De boss must have been some kin' of sargint in de war, on account he alway dress so neat."

One time James shared the front seat of the pickup with my father and Pat on the long trip to the up-country shoot. This was unusual, and James found himself wedged in between Pat and Daddy. He had a huge wad of Red Dog chewing tobacco in his cheek and nowhere to spit, being too intimidated to ask them to stop the car so he could get out. He got sicker and sicker, and he told me later: "I was too glad I be a color' man, so de Boss couldn't see me greenin' up. I like to bust wide open before we arrive. Ooh, I was *too* sick!"

Another time, again riding up-country, James had a bad headache and Pat gave him an Alka-Seltzer. He didn't know you had to drop the tablet in a glass of water, so "I jus' chew it up and pretty soon it commence to fizz, and the fizz come out my nose and my mout' and my ear." James had a wonderful sense of humor and he loved a joke, even if it was on himself.

Silver Hill after Restoration

My mother loved to laugh with the men, and they reminisce about the time they were watching while she had her picture taken with three of her proper lady house guests, all sitting seriously on the front porch, wearing full beards of Spanish moss. She was not above giving the men a complicit wink when Daddy was scolding them about something.

*Mummy (center) and friends*

The house parties in those days were great fun, and I could hear the grownups' laughter echoing from the dining room all the way back to my nursery wing. Many guests came from Philadelphia and New York. The men were all quail and duck hunters, and their wives were sporty types who enjoyed the life. Looking through the guest book I see the signatures of many perennials like the Watson Webbs. He was sour and grumpy, and she was a dedicated collector of American Folk Art. They were both wonderful shots; Mrs. Webb even held the record for a giant Kodiak bear. Cousin Liv—Livingston Biddle—wrote long complimentary verses in the guest book. The family's best friend, Mr. Kline ("Kliney") was a yearly visitor. We children loved Mr. Francis Richmond, a bachelor with a loud jolly haw-haw laugh, who used to get down on the floor and play raucous games of "Pit" with us, luring us into the forbidden parlor.

Mr. Charlie Cadwalader came every year. He was supposed to be on the wagon but managed to pour half a decanter of sherry in his turtle soup. Mr. Robert Goelet got tipsy and wrote suggestive remarks to my mother in the guest book. Tall awkward Mr. Joe Lippincott, the Philadelphia publisher, collected tree-snail shells and kept pet crows at his home in Philadelphia. He gave me one, named Joe Crow, and told me a funny story about how one of his crows hated his mother-in-law. The crow used to glide silently down behind her when she was drinking iced tea on the porch and peck her ankles.

Mr. Arthur Meigs, the short-tempered architect of the Friendfield restoration, was an annual visitor, and not-so-secretly in love with my mother. She enjoyed the attention but never reciprocated, as was the frustrating case for all her admirers. Another of these was Mr. George Widener, who remained devoted until her death. I remember he called on her after her stroke, and I saw tears in his eyes when I gave him the message from my bedridden mother that "I don't want him to see me when I am like this." He left the house bowed with grief.

My family had many friends who owned neighboring plantations, but they would usually only visit for lunch, or cookouts in the woods before the quail hunts, as the driving distances were too great. At that time, in the thirties, Yankees like the DuPonts, the Paul Millses, the Robert Montgomerys, the Goelets, the Beaches, the Iselins, the Emersons, the Vanderbilts and the Guggenheims bought up many of the old places, rescuing them from decrepitude. There was no money in the South after the Civil War, and the locals didn't resent the newcomers as deeply as you might think. They loved their homeland and were pleased that the old places were being saved because it was impossible in those hard times for the original owners to keep them up. The Yankee presence brought in new money and created jobs in that depressed rural community. (Today, the situation is reversed, and the plantations are once more owned and enjoyed by Southerners, or made into golf courses and gated communities.)

In the early thirties, Winston Churchill visited his old friend Bernard Baruch at nearby Hobcaw Barony, and a luncheon was given for him at which the champagne flowed. My parents were invited and Mummy was seated next to Churchill. He was at his amusing best, and she was entranced. She avoided Daddy's eye and his broad hints that it was time to go home. The brandy made its rounds, prolonging the lunch, to the annoyance of my teetotal father. Afterwards he remained skeptical about Churchill for a long time, until World War II. "Damned drunk," Daddy dismissed the great man. Was he jealous? I suppose so, although it was not the first time my mother had captivated a man at a party.

Another famous visitor to Hobcaw was President Franklin D. Roosevelt. His private railroad car was scheduled to drop him off at the Atlantic Coastline railroad spur that passed by the front gate of Friendfield. Tom Joiner, the huntsman, happened to be riding his bike down the driveway when "all dem army mens in uniform popped out de bushes, and dey order me to hol' up me hans and stop right there. I thought sho' enough the War had dun come to Georgetown!"

The story goes that on one of his trips, Mr. Roosevelt brought along a guest, Lucy Mercer Rutherford, who was officially Mrs. Roosevelt's secretary at the White House, but also President Roosevelt's mistress in her spare time. A few days later, Eleanor Roosevelt paid a surprise visit. Mrs. Rutherford was rushed out the back door, just as the First Lady arrived at the front, and scandal was averted.

In the spring, three or four of the shooting ponies were moved down to the small whitewashed stable near the marsh and cypress swamp at the far end of the lawn. My friends and I were allowed to ride by ourselves, but catching the ponies in the corral was a hard job. The little horses were pigheaded, and wheeled away from us, kicking up puffs of sand and dust. They hated opening their mouths for the bit, clenching their long yellow teeth, and we were too short to force the bridle up over their pinned-back ears.

Just as we despaired, kindly James Graham, who was watching out for us all the time, came to the rescue. The minute the horses saw him shaking a pan of oats, they would become tractable, and he saddled them up for us, tightening the girths with mighty heaves, while the ponies tried to swell up their stomachs against the constricting pressure.

Off we trotted from the corral, cap pistols at the ready, armed to the teeth with rolls of red caps that smelt pungently of gunpowder when we fired at each other. We cantered along sandy roads through the woods, the green tops of the pines contrasting with a blue Carolina sky. The sun was warm on our backs, yellow and blue butterflies fluttered over bright green ferns, purple violets and wild flag, and the unshod hooves of our horses plopped softly in the sand.

A favorite destination was Tompkins Store next to the highway, about a mile down the front drive. It was a ramshackle frame building, and a rusty tin *Drink Coca-Cola* sign hung lopsidedly above the front porch. A few old white men sat outside on wooden kitchen chairs, a-whittlin' and a-spittin', and after they watched us tying up the ponies to spindly gum trees, they returned to their pastime without comment, except for a "How you'all?" and a wave.

Inside there was a beat-up wooden counter and a few stools, presided over by red-faced bristly Mr. Tompkins, who leaned over to beam down on us with rheumy eyes, spraying us with his pungent breath. "What'll be yore pleasure, little lady? Great God, amighty, ain't you all sumpin' to be ridin' all this way from home. Mighty glad to greet you on this lovely day!"

We drank warmish sodas from murky Coca-Cola glasses, feeling very independent as we searched for the coins to pay. Then ZAP! Without warning and to our everlasting admiration, Mr. Tompkins squirted a juicy jet of dark brown tobacco juice across the counter. It landed with an accurate pinging splat in the brass spittoon in the corner, just missing my head on its way.

Now we understood the full richness of our jingle sung to the aria from *Carmen*. *"Toreador-a don't spit on the floor, Use the cuspidor, that's what it's for."*

"You'all hurry back now, you hear?" drawled Mr. T., and we rode on back home, practicing our hawking and messy spitting, amid gales of giggles.

Another expedition was to the foundation of an old abandoned fish-processing plant, "The Fish Factory," which was flooded with river water and covered with bright green algae scum. Once, two huge alligators were trapped in there near a half-submerged, bloated, hairy carcass of a deer. They floated on the surface with just their snouts and eye ridges showing. The smell was sickening. We threw in a branch, the gators dove with a terrifying WHUMP! of their scaly tails, the horses shied and tried to bolt, and we fled for our lives.

The iron mouths of the ponies never responded to the fiercest sawing tugs, and almost always, one or another of us got run away with on the way home. Normally they were only ridden in the winter for quail shooting, hardly ever faster than a walk, and so they were delighted with the chance to run, especially when heading for the barn. They hadn't finished shedding their winter coats yet; the sweat foamed up under the girths, and gobs of hair stuck to the wet saddle blankets.

We arrived back at the stable breathless and scared that we would get into trouble with Mummy and Daddy, who had ordered us not to bring the horses home hot. But James never told on us, and the ponies didn't seem to be the worse for it.

We left the blankets and tack to dry on the corral fence and came back to the house, smelling pungently of horse; dirty, hot, and excited to relate the various happenings on the ride, like getting "lost," nearly falling off, maybe sighting a snake or a hawk or a wild pig and being scared to death by the gators.

The night coon hunt was our favorite adventure of all. After supper, which for once, we were allowed to eat without changing out of blue jeans, we were boosted into the back of Pat's pickup, and went jouncing off into the mysterious dark.

A bright moon pooled brilliant white light on the forest floor between the etched black shadows of the live oaks. The hounds were released from their cages in the back of the dog truck and went crashing off toward the Port's Creek swamp, sounding a confused medley of barks and yips and deep-throated howls. The air smelt of pine, mud and wildness, and the men whooped and hollered encouragement to their dogs: "Speak to him, Rock!" Or Stranger or Queenie, or whichever hound belonged to him. "Listening at de dawgs" was like hearing an unfolding story. Some hounds were silent trailers until they barked "treed," and others bayed as soon as they struck a hot trail. The men knew each dog's voice individually, which stage of the chase he was signaling and what type of game—coon, bobcat, or deer—he was trailing, and they likened it to music. It was bad if the dogs ran a deer, because the hounds would seldom obey, some-times staying away for days, swimming the creeks and even the river, risking being eaten by the ever-hopeful alligators.

When they struck a fresh scent, Pat blew a long mellow blast on his hunting horn—a cow horn with a bit of hide still on, and no mouthpiece. None of us could ever make a sound come out of it, even though we blew till our cheeks popped.

Then we were off, running through thorny brush and cane swamp, rubber boots squelching, following the faint light of the lantern or flashlight way ahead. "Don't go thataway, that thicket's so thick a dawg would have to back up to bark! Come around hyar, watch for the ravine." Breathlessly we staggered on, until…"He's treed, he's treed!" someone would yell, as the dogs' barking rhythm changed to a sharp frantic staccato. When we caught up, the dogs would be leap-ing at the tree trunk, trying desperately to climb after their quarry, biting off chunks of bark, looking like mad hounds of hell in the flickering light.

And up there, hunched on a high branch, was the furry masked raccoon, picked out by the beam of a powerful flashlight. "Shine his eyes, shine his eyes!" and his bright little eyes reflected the beam. The designated shooter aimed, while someone shouted, "Pop him in de haid." A sharp crack of the .22 rifle, a smell of powder, and after a desperate clinging delay, the doomed coon came crashing down through the branches into the snapping fighting melee of bloodthirsty hounds.

After a yell of "Stretch 'im, boys," the dogs were whipped off, and the raccoon was dropped into a gunnysack to be skinned and served up for someone's Sunday roast. The hill raccoons that fed on acorns were prized, unlike the carrion-eating possum, or the marsh coons that ate fishes and frogs.

Another time a coon took refuge in a hollow halfway up a gum tree. "We'll have to smoke him out," said Pat, as the dogs jumped and tore at the bark. "What we goin' smoke him wit?" asked Junior. "Take off your shirt," said Pat, "and climb up there to that holler. Wrap your shirt around this stick and set it afire, and poke it down that hole."

We watched anxiously, as the shirt burned to blackened scraps, the dogs became wild with suspense, and nothing emerged. Junior slid back down, shivering in his undershirt. "Grab de axe, boy, and we'll chop her down!" Junior went to work with the axe on the tree trunk and when the tree was nearly severed, Pat—who loved having the last word—demanded the axe, and delivered the final mighty whack, after Junior had done all the work. Out scrambled the coon, slightly singed, into the melee of barking dogs, and that was that. Pat would go to any lengths to capture any game.

On one of the hunts the hounds killed a possum, which was then considered a prime predator against quail. "Look at this," Pat told us, and with a forefinger he scooped seven tiny squirming, hairless, pink babies out of the mother possum's pouch. In front of our horrified eyes, he stepped on them, commenting, "They would have died anyway." Hard to take for two northern girls like Minnie and me, and we never forgot that shocking moment. Life in the woods, and nature itself, is brutal. "People who talk about the Cathedral of the Woods ain't never been there in real life," an old timer once told me disgustedly.

Pat's wife Jessie told me that once she and her husband were driving to a wedding, all dressed up. Pat was wearing a white suit, and he spotted a possum by the side of the road. He screeched the car to a halt, grabbed his ever-present rifle, leaped out, and shot it, spattering his good clothes with mud and blood. Jessie was appalled and read him the riot act, but nothing ever changed him. Hunting was his passion.

Reflecting on those hunts today, it seems like cruel sport, only partially justified by remembering that raccoons and possums and wildcats were then thought to be major predators upon the quail population. In fact wildlife researchers have now established that snakes are actually the biggest consumers of quail eggs.

The men from that part of the South were all hunters born and bred, brought up with a gun from the earliest age. Hunting and fishing were a way of life. The wives baked wonderful biscuits and cakes, participated in church events and taught their daughters to be Southern ladies. It was all part of my childhood, and I loved it, although I was much more of a tomboy than a "little lady." On vacations when I was watching James or Tom skin a coon, and learning not to be scared of snakes, my friends at home were going to parties, to museums, and on ski trips.

Looking back, I wouldn't trade my experiences at Friendfield for anything, although when I was a teenager I remember staying awake on New Year's Eve, enviously listening to the countdown from Times Square on my radio, waiting for the ball to drop that traditionally ushered in the New Year. My mother and father had gone up to bed at nine-thirty as usual. "When you wake up, you'll be a whole year older," they said annually. This was no comfort at all for missing the fun I was sure that my friends were having at their parties.

As a youngster I was nearly unaware of the harsh realities emphasized by Charles Joyner, as quoted in a book about the Gullah people of Johns Island, South Carolina:[1]

> *The policy was called segregation, or Jim Crow. It was very thoroughgoing, and behind the mask of civility our harsh racial caste system branded all Black South Carolinians as inferior.*
>
> *Segregation was characterized by two sets of almost everything; one set of churches, stores, funeral homes, toilets, drinking fountains for black Carolinians, and another for white Carolinians.*
>
> *Black students were relegated to Jim Crow schools, black travelers to the back of the Jim Crow bus, black moviegoers to the Jim Crow balcony, and there were separate neighborhoods for blacks and whites.*
>
> *It was not difficult to tell which were which: the pavement ended where the black neighborhoods began. But not everything came in pairs. Some things such as parks, libraries and swimming pools were rarely available to black Carolinians at all.*

My own opinion, however, after much reflection is that the hardships of Reconstruction, which gravely affected both blacks and whites, forged a common bond between the races in spite of these abuses. In the rural South today, there still exists a courtesy and understanding between blacks and whites that is rarely found in Northern cities. The shared heritage of farming and hunting, the armed

---

1.    Carawan, Guy and Candie, *Ain't you got a right to the tree of life?*

services, and strong religious faith brought the races closer together. Although the civil rights movement created legal equality, and the problems of the past are lessening, troubles are by no means over. Education and jobs are the key to true racial equality. There is still de facto segregation today, although in the Georgetown Historical District, homes belonging to both races have been found on the same streets since post-Civil War days.

Friendfield Plantation and its environment created a lasting influence on me and my children and grandchildren. Country wisdom, colorful humor, the importance of family ties, courtesy, patriotism, the rewards of hard work, and the love of nature—these have been its enduring gifts. My family understands and deeply appreciates this powerful attachment. It is our good fortune to have added Southern values to our Yankee heritage.

# *Epilogue*

So there they are, these memories of my happy and fortunate childhood, growing up in the 1930's. They are unusual for my ignorance about sex, and unquestioning obedience to the Victorian-Edwardian manners and strictures of the day. It was a childhood dominated by sentiment, by family, by well-loved houses, country environments and fun.

Afterwards, off came the rose-colored glasses and the real world began. But that's another story.

*Frances Train*
*Bedford, New York 2006*

978-0-595-40968-6
0-595-40968-7